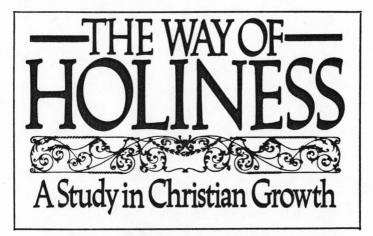

THE WAY OF —
HOLINESS

A Study in Christian Growth

Kenneth Prior

InterVarsity Press
Downers Grove
Illinois 60515

D1316761

InterVarsity Press is the book-publishing division of Inter-Varsity Christian Fellowship, a student movement active on campus at hundreds of universities, colleges and schools of nursing. For information about local and regional activities, write IVCF, 233 Langdon St., Madison, WI 53703.

Distributed in Canada through InterVarsity Press, 1875 Leslie St., Unit 10, Don Mills, Ontario M3B 2M5, Canada.

All quotations from the Scriptures, unless otherwise noted, are from the Revised Standard Version of the Bible, copyrighted 1946, 1952, © 1971, 1973 by the Division of Christian Education of the National Council of the Churches of Christ in the USA, and used by permission.

Cover photograph: Robert Cushman Hayes

ISBN 0-87784-380-5

Printed in the United States of America

Library of Congress Cataloging in Publication Data

Prior, Kenneth Francis William.
  The way of holiness.

  Includes bibliographical references.
  1. Sanctification. I. Title.
BT765.P7 1982   234'.8   82-16214
ISBN 0-87784-380-5

17 16 15 14 13 12 11 10 9 8 7 6 5 4 3 2 1
95 94 93 92 91 90 89 88 87 86 85 84 83 82

Preface

It has given me considerable pleasure to work on this revision of *The Way of Holiness* and to take advantage of the many helpful suggestions I have received since it was first published. Some have commented on the many quotations I have made from past writers. On a subject like this I feel that it is important to learn from the great biblical exponents of the past, such as John Owen with his practical wisdom. We also need to learn from past mistakes; failure to do so is the reason why they constantly recur, and why the theme of this book never ceases to be relevant.

Since the first edition we have seen the worldwide growth of the charismatic movement. It is a big subject, which is largely outside the scope of this book and on which much has been written, so I have restricted my comments to what is relevant to holiness and sanctification. Expressions such as "renewal" and "the fullness of the Holy Spirit," for example, must be understood in their scriptural sense to avoid confusion.

I owe much to many teachers—past writers and present friends—whose advice I have treasured.

Kenneth F. W. Prior
May 1982

1
The
Way of
Holiness

The life God plans for his people is described by Isaiah as "the Way of Holiness" (Is 35:8 NIV). But what is holiness? For many people, the word, if it conveys anything at all, revives memories of stained-glass windows depicting pale and unhealthy-looking faces with bones clearly visible under a thin layer of flesh! It reminds us of hair shirts and other things designed to ensure that life not be too enjoyable. And always present, of course, is the halo to underline how far the whole idea is from the realities of the twentieth century.

But is this really what the Bible means by the word *holiness*? Far from it. The holy people of the Bible are miles removed from such popular misconceptions. Instead of their being anemic, they are tough with sunburnt faces, like Elijah,

John the Baptist and even our Lord himself. Instead of being miserable, they are joyful, like Paul, the great apostle to the Gentiles, whose happiness was so deep and lasting that he could sing even in a filthy Roman prison. Instead of being distinguished from ordinary people by an unearthly halo, the early Christians mixed with all types of humanity, from the publicans and sinners of the Gospels, and the "fatherless and widows" of the Epistle of James, to "the saints... of Caesar's household" (Phil 4:22).

The Attraction of Holiness

Holiness, rightly understood, is an attractive quality. James Philip rightly observes: "The greatest saints of God have been characterized, not by haloes and an atmosphere of distant unapproachability, but by their humanity. They have been intensely human and lovable people with a twinkle in their eyes. One has only to read the biographies of men like Moody, or Spurgeon, or Hudson Taylor, to see how true this is."[1] Holiness, then, is a practical concept, and has to do with our present earthly life rather than with some future, heavenly existence (*glorification* is the word for that). The holy person reveals here and now a sense of purpose and victory. C.H. Spurgeon, the great nineteenth-century preacher, once said:

> It would be a great pity if in the process of being qualified for the next life, we become disqualified for this; but it is not so. It would be a very strange thing if, in order to be fit for the company of angels, we should grow unfit to associate with men; but it is not so. It would be a singular circumstance if those who speak of heaven have nothing to say concerning the way thither; but it is not so. ... True religion has as much to do with this world as with the world to come; it is always urging us onward to the higher and better life; but it does so by processes and precepts which fit us worthily to spend our days while here below.[2]

Now it is with these processes and precepts, as Spurgeon calls them, that the doctrine of sanctification is concerned.

Although in English there are two groups of words, *holy* and *holiness* on the one hand and *sanctify, sanctification* and *saint* on the other, in both Hebrew and Greek the words which these words translate are all derived from one root.[3] Christian theology has always regarded these words as expressing one of the basic doctrines underlying the Christian life. Sanctification has been the heading under which various aspects of the Christian life have been placed. Growth in grace, victory over sin and the present work of the Holy Spirit in the heart of the believer, transforming his or her nature, are among them. If we want a clear summary of the range of truth included in sanctification, it is hard to improve on the definition given in the Westminster Catechism, the statement of doctrine officially held by Presbyterian churches. Sanctification is said to be "the work of God's free grace, whereby we are renewed in the whole man after the image of God, and are enabled more and more to die unto sin, and live unto righteousness."

All this is in keeping with biblical usage. In 1 Thessalonians 5, for example, Paul gives a number of directives for Christian living and then summarizes, "May the God of peace himself sanctify you wholly" (1 Thess 5:23). To quote John Owen's comment on this verse, "The reason hereof is, because all the graces and duties which he had enjoined, belonged to their sanctification."[4] Peter, too, makes holiness a basic factor of the Christian life which finds its application in the various commands of God. He tells us "Be holy yourselves in all your conduct" (1 Pet 1:15). Just as *uncleanness* is a word for the life of sin, so *holiness* is a word for the life of faith; it includes all the positive virtue that God intends.

The Mark of a Christian
Holiness, therefore, is the characteristic mark of a Christian.

It is one of the chief purposes of our election, for "he chose us in him before the foundation of the world, that we should be holy and blameless before him" (Eph 1:4). Or, as Paul put it when writing to the Romans, "Whom he foreknew he also predestined to be conformed to the image of his Son" (Rom 8:29). Moreover it is commanded for every Christian without distinction. It is to all members of the church and not to the members of some special religious order that the apostle writes: "This is the will of God, your sanctification" (1 Thess 4:3).

This misconception—that holiness is intended for the elite within the church—often goes with the stained-glass window ideas. It is an attitude usually associated with the Roman Catholic Church, but by no means confined to it. Are not many Christians dominated by a tacit assumption that there are two standards of Christian commitment, one for missionaries and a lower one for ordinary Christians? We expect missionaries to sacrifice money, comfort and even marriage in pursuit of their calling. But it is different for the rest of us. Or is it? Is this a biblical attitude?

Certainly not. Nowhere does Scripture suggest such a double standard. When Paul, for example, was addressing the Christians at Corinth, he did not say: "Saint Paul to the Christians at Corinth," but "Paul, called by the will of God to be an apostle . . . to those sanctified in Christ Jesus, called to be saints" (1 Cor 1:1-2). He did not use the name *saint* exclusively for himself and those like him, but applied it to all the members of the church in Corinth. And, as the rest of the Epistle makes clear, this included some who had not progressed far in the life of sanctification. All alike are called to be saints.

The pursuit of holiness, then, is one of the supreme quests in which a Christian is to be engaged. We are not primarily to seek happiness, although this will come our way as a byproduct, as Jesus himself promised: "Happy are those who are hungry and thirsty for goodness, for they will be fully satisfied!" (Mt 5:6 Phillips). Holiness must come first. It is essential to salvation. "Strive for... the holiness without which no one will see the Lord" (Heb 12:14). No one who is careless about this is entitled to any assurance of salvation. Indeed, it would be presumptuous to imagine that we could enjoy forgiveness and eternal life without any intention to be made holy. So attention to the way of holiness is one of the most important means by which "to confirm your call and election" (2 Pet 1:10).

2
The
Holiness
of God

A*ny study of sanctification* ought to begin with the holiness of God. Holiness is primarily a divine attribute and is referred to in the Old Testament more than all the other attributes of God put together. Because God is holy he commands his creatures to be holy. The command, "You shall be holy; for I the LORD your God am holy" (Lev 19:2), is the basis for this doctrine in the Bible. God first reveals himself to his people as essentially holy; then he proceeds to demand the same from them. So fundamental is this principle to Christian living that Peter bases on it his appeal to his readers to live differently now that they are Christians (1 Pet 1:14-16). We cannot stress too strongly that the supreme motive is not that holiness is a means of happiness or peace of mind, but that it is an obligation placed upon us by one who is himself holy.

But holiness in the Christian believer is not only the result of a command. If it were, there would be small likelihood of us sinners becoming in any degree holy. Christian holiness arises out of our relationship with a holy God. We are "partakers of the divine nature" (2 Pet 1:4) or, as the writer to the Hebrews puts it, we "share his holiness" (Heb 12:10). In other words, holiness is not only commanded by God's law, but is made available by his grace.

The Westminster Catechism recognizes that divine holiness is the essential background to the believer's sanctification. It describes sanctification as the process of being "renewed in the whole man after the image of God." In sanctification God is fulfilling his original creative purpose, which was to "make man in our image" (Gen 1:26). His ultimate aim is to make people like himself. That is, sanctification is concerned with promoting *godliness*, a word which has sadly disappeared from the vocabulary of many Christians.

God's Holiness Defined

What do we mean when we describe God as holy? To define this is no easy matter. Mercifully, a complete investigation into the various definitions which have been advanced is beyond the scope of this book. Instead, we shall content ourselves with a grasp of the basic idea, keeping in mind that our ultimate objective is a practical one: to discover the way of holy living that God intends for his people.

First, what is the literal meaning of the words *holy* and *sanctify*? Unlike most words in the Bible, they are exclusively religious. They are used only where God and his will for the lives of his people are in view. Although no one knows for sure the meaning of the Hebrew root, the majority think that it is a Semitic one which means "to cut," and so conveys the idea of "to separate" or "to set apart." So when God is described as holy it means that he is separated from his creation and exalted above it. He is, to quote Isaiah 57:15, "the high and lofty One who inhabits eternity, whose name is Holy." Furthermore, he is distinct from his creatures; no one may be compared with him. Again, we use the words of Isaiah: "To whom then will you compare me, that I should be like him? says the Holy One" (Is 40:25). False gods lack this quality of holiness, as Moses recognized when he exclaimed: "Who is like thee, O LORD, among the gods? Who is like thee, majestic in holiness?" (Ex 15:11).

Although for convenience the holiness of God is often grouped in theological textbooks with his so-called moral attributes such as his righteousness, love and mercy, it is rather a master attribute which includes all the others in their perfection. For what is it that renders God so utterly different from his creatures and so elevated above them but his perfection in these attributes: his perfect goodness, his unquenchable zeal for righteousness, the boundlessness of his love, the limitless power which he wields, and his infinite wisdom and understanding? To say he is holy is just another way of saying he is God. Indeed, in the Old Testament God is sometimes simply designated "the Holy One."

All this was emphasized in Rudolf Otto's important book, translated into English under the title *The Idea of the Holy*.[1] Otto shows that holiness is no mere negative concept, but the most essential ingredient in the very nature of God, for which he coined the term *the Numinous*. It produces a sense that one is in the presence of something strange and unfamiliar. This is how C. S. Lewis explains it:

> Those who have not met this term may be introduced to it by the following device. Suppose you were told there was a tiger in the next room: you would know that you were in danger and would probably feel fear. But if you were told "There is a ghost in the next room," and believed it, you would feel, indeed, what is often called fear, but of a dif-

ferent kind. It would not be based on the knowledge of danger, for no one is primarily afraid of what a ghost may do to him, but of the mere fact that it is a ghost. It is "uncanny" rather than dangerous, and the special kind of fear it excites may be called Dread. With the Uncanny one has reached the fringes of the Numinous. Now suppose that you were told simply "There is a mighty spirit in the room," and believed it. Your feelings would then be even less like the mere fear of danger: but the disturbance would be profound. You would feel wonder and a certain shrinking—a sense of inadequacy to cope with such a visitant and of prostration before it—an emotion which might be expressed in Shakespeare's words "Under it my genius is rebuked." This feeling may be described as awe, and the object which excites it as the *Numinous*.[2]

The Holiness of God and Sin
Although we have not yet seen in the idea of holiness any ethical content, Christianity certainly teaches that God is separated from his creatures and elevated above them largely because of their sin. Not every religion recognizes this. As Stephen Neill points out:

The idea that holiness could exist without ethical virtue has become completely strange to us. It is well to remember that this may be true of us, but it is not everywhere and universally true. In India, for example, both religion and ethics exist, but the unbreakable connection between them has never yet been made. It is possible for an earnest Hindu to seek contact with the "holy" . . . to attain to a very deep sense of the "numinous," to feel that he has been in touch with the *mysterium tremendum*, and yet not to be convinced that such an experience need be in any way related to a demand for ethical righteousness, or that the experience, if attained, need necessarily have any direct effect on his moral conduct in the future.[3]

That holiness applies to sin is, however, clearly recognized in the Bible. The prophet Habakkuk, for example, having addressed God as "my Holy One," continues, "Thou who art of purer eyes than to behold evil and canst not look on wrong" (Hab 1:13). With these words in mind, R. A. Finlayson has described holiness as "a general term for the moral excellence of God, and His freedom from all moral limitations in His moral perfection... a declaration expressive of the moral sensitiveness of God, shrinking from all evil and sin."[4]

All this means that God cannot compromise with sin in any form. He must demand conformity with his moral laws, and anyone who would have dealings with him must be pure in thought, word and deed. "Who shall ascend the hill of the LORD? And who shall stand in his holy place?" asks the psalmist. Back comes the reply: "He who has clean hands and a pure heart, who does not lift up his soul to what is false, and does not swear deceitfully" (Ps 24:3-4). To summarize in the words of Berkhof: "This ethical holiness of God may be defined as that perfection of God, in virtue of which He eternally wills and maintains His own moral excellence, abhors sin, and demands purity in His moral creatures."[5]

When people fail to fulfill these requirements, God's holiness demands that he express his displeasure in wrath and judgment (see, e.g., Is 5:16). It is not surprising, then, if people faced with such a God sense their own sin and unworthiness. They would be like Isaiah who, having seen the Lord "high and lifted up," and having heard the "Holy, holy, holy" of the seraphim, confessed: "Woe is me! For I am lost; for I am a man of unclean lips, and I dwell in the midst of a people of unclean lips; for my eyes have seen the King, the LORD of hosts!" (Is 6:5).

Our Response to God's Holiness
How does all this bear on our subject? It has a very profound bearing, for not only does it help to show us what holiness is,

19

but it also gives us the supreme ground for our holiness. If we are to become holy, we must face the challenge of God's holiness. We must "sanctify the LORD of hosts himself" (Is 8:13 KJV), that is, acknowledge him to be holy. This is what is expressed in the familiar words of the Lord's Prayer, "hallowed be Thy Name," for *hallow* is the same word as *sanctify* in Greek. Peter quotes these words of Isaiah with some significant modifications. Not only does he apply them to Christ, but he significantly adds "in your hearts" (1 Pet 3:15). We are to recognize the holiness of God, not merely by the profession of our lips, but in the submission of our hearts.[6] If Christians are to avoid compromising their standards in the midst of opposition, then from the very center of their beings there must be this awesome attitude toward God in his holiness.

Now the word used in Scripture for this attitude is *fear*. As our quotation from Isaiah 8:13 (KJV) says, "Sanctify the LORD of hosts himself; and let him be your fear, and let him be your dread." This is no slavish, cowering emotion, but the healthy attitude of awe and reverence which befits the holiness of God. It is the reverence and godly fear which the writer to the Hebrews sees as a necessary accompaniment of the kind of service God requires (Heb 12:28 KJV). If holiness is the supreme attribute of God, then reverence must be correspondingly paramount in his people's attitude toward him. This reverence has been significantly defined by the psychologist William McDougall as "the religious emotion *par excellence;* few merely human powers are capable of exciting reverence, this blend of wonder, fear, gratitude, and negative self-feeling."[7]

Now the fear of the Lord has a great deal to do with the way in which a Christian lives. Paul, for example, urges us to "make holiness perfect in the fear of God" (2 Cor 7:1). The book of Proverbs teaches the practical importance of fearing God, as the following quotations demonstrate:

The fear of the LORD is the beginning of knowledge. (1:7)
The fear of the LORD is hatred of evil. (8:13)
In the fear of the LORD one has strong confidence. (14:26)
The fear of the LORD is a fountain of life. (14:27)
By the fear of the LORD a man avoids evil. (16:6)
Yet the importance of reverence and fear toward God in relation to sanctification is not always recognized. Surely one of the reasons in these days for low moral standards is the lack of awareness of the majesty and holiness of God and of our accountability toward him. To a certain degree the same deficiencies can be seen among professing Christians. One of the marks of spiritual decline is that "there is no fear of God before his eyes" (Ps 36:1). Instead we fill ourselves with confidence in our own sufficiency. This is the complete antithesis of holiness.

3
A
Holy
People

As *we have seen, it is because* God is holy that he calls upon his people to be holy. What does it mean then for people to be holy and to share in what is essentially a divine attribute? To move from the holiness of the almighty and eternal God to holiness in finite and earthbound people is a big jump. We will use therefore, as a steppingstone for our understanding, what the Bible teaches about the holiness of places, objects and times.

Holiness of Places and Objects
Places may be described as holy when they become the scene of an awareness of God's presence and hence the occasion of awe and wonder. Such places become unapproachable because they are set apart and different from others. Most peo-

ple are barred from drawing near at all, while those who may are entitled to do so only on certain conditions. For example, strict regulations governed the entering of the high priest into the holy of holies once a year.

Another helpful example of a holy place is the burning bush where Moses was told, "The place on which you are standing is holy ground" (Ex 3:5). The place had become so associated with God himself that it too was holy. Even Moses was allowed to draw near only after he had removed his shoes. Like the holiness of God himself, so the holiness of objects and places has both positive and negative aspects. Positively, the places are set apart for God while, negatively, any who would mar them must be excluded.

Examples abound in the Old Testament of objects being regarded as holy. We may cite the vessels and furnishings of the Tabernacle and the Temple (see, e.g., Ex 40:10-11). Here again the same two aspects surface. Positively, the things were set apart for the service and worship of God while negatively they were set apart from all other use and had to be ceremonially cleansed before they were worthy of the purpose for which they were intended.

Days too may be holy. The Sabbath was to be kept holy because it was a day especially belonging to God.[1] And if the day was to be devoted to God, it had to be freed from the activities with which people were occupied on the other six days.

Holiness in People

These examples help us to understand one aspect of holiness in people. When they were appointed to special office under the old economy, people too were sanctified. Here the word is not being used in any ethical sense. It was not that they had reached some particular degree of moral attainment and were necessarily any less sinful than others. Indeed, one could be a sacred person and yet completely lacking in spiritual life and character. This is amply demonstrated in the Old Testament.

The New Testament has similar ways of speaking when it refers to holy prophets and holy apostles. It is in this sense that we speak of the apostles as "Saint Paul," "Saint John" and so on. They were set apart for the special office of being an apostle, which for them involved, among other things, the privilege and responsibility of being the human writers of Holy Scripture.[2] It was no doubt in a similar sense that our Lord applied this to himself when he prayed, "For their sakes I sanctify myself, that they also might be sanctified through the truth" (Jn 17:19 KJV). He was not purging himself from any evil which had previously been present, but he was setting himself apart for the work of redemption, which meant both positive dedication to all that it involved and separation from everything that would hinder.

But holiness is also laid as an obligation on all God's people. The description of God's people as holy was made first of Israel, who enjoyed the privilege of being God's "own possession among all peoples . . . and a holy nation" (Ex 19:5-6). Peter uses the same language of the Christian church (1 Pet 2:9). So when he puts before his readers the challenge of God's holiness, he addresses it not just to those called to special office, but to the entire congregation he is writing (1 Pet 1:15-16). Just as "I am holy" summarizes all that goes to make God what he is, so the command "You shall be holy" lays before God's people what is to be their distinctive characteristic. Just as a place associated with God becomes holy, with all the precautions and demands which that makes, so must a person be holy who would have dealings with the Holy One. Little wonder the Hebrew Christians are challenged to "strive for . . . the holiness without which no one will see the Lord" (Heb 12:14). Indeed, when we consider the Final Judgment we see that in the last analysis there are only two classes of people, the holy and the unholy. Notice the finality with which this is expressed in the last chapter of the Bible. "Let the evildoer still do evil, and the filthy still be filthy, and the righteous still do right, and the holy still be holy" (Rev 22:11).

The negative aspect of holiness. The first reaction of people who are challenged by God's holiness and the demands it makes upon them is an awareness of their unworthiness. The holiness of God has been likened to a bright, searching light which ruthlessly shows up all that is impure and unclean. When Isaiah had his vision of the holiness of God, he was immediately prostrated with a sense of his own sin. In trying to open his mouth, he realized that the very lips with which he spoke were morally unclean. He saw the hopelessness of his position, and all he could say for himself was "Woe is me!" (Is 6:5).

Peter had a similar experience. He saw our Lord at work and heard his teaching. He must have caught a glimpse of God's holiness expressed in the perfection with which Jesus went about his task, for "he fell down at Jesus' knees, saying, 'Depart from me, for I am a sinful man, O Lord' " (Lk 5:8). This reaction to God's holiness is the only one that befits a sinner, and if, in spite of our sin, we are to be the people of a holy God, then we are impelled to share his abhorrence of our sin. The call to holiness is a call to come out on God's side of the gulf that separates him from our sin. This will mean separating ourselves from everything that is sinful and unworthy, for cleanness in thought, word and deed is demanded of all those who would approach God.

Holiness is demanded of people when they are praying, for prayer is to be pursued "lifting holy hands" (1 Tim 2:8). When Isaiah censured God's people for their lack of holiness, he went on to expose the uselessness of their prayers while in that condition: "When you spread forth your hands, I will hide my eyes from you; even though you make many prayers, I will not listen; your hands are full of blood" (Is 1:15). The remedy is obvious: "Wash yourselves; make yourselves clean; remove the evil of your doings from before my eyes; cease to do evil, learn to do good; seek justice, correct oppression; defend the fatherless, plead for the widow" (Is 1:16-17).

We have to remember, too, that the life of holiness has to be lived in the midst of a world that has been marred and ruined by sin. Christian holiness will dictate a way of life utterly different from other people's way of living. This point is repeatedly made in the Old Testament. It was on the ground of holiness that the Israelites were forbidden to follow the customs of the tribes around them (Deut 12:1-19). They were not allowed to take spouses from pagan tribes. In the New Testament the standard is no lower. Christians are to maintain the same distinctiveness as their Old Testament counterparts. Addressing Christians living in a typical pagan city of the ancient world, Paul writes: "Therefore come out from them, and be separate from them, says the Lord, and touch nothing unclean; then I will welcome you" (2 Cor 6:17).

In view of all this, any study of sanctification must be largely occupied with sin and how it is overcome. If holiness is to be perfected in us, we must cleanse ourselves from "every defilement of body and spirit" (2 Cor 7:1). This negative aspect of holiness cannot be avoided. Not only are the Ten Commandments expressed as prohibitions, but even when Paul extols the positive virtue love, he lists what love does not do (1 Cor 13:4-6). So in the following chapters we shall be considering the nature of sin, the extent of the damage it has caused and God's answer to it. Before we do this, however, we must see the positive side of holiness. We must never lose sight of this.

The positive aspect of holiness.   Holiness is much more than just avoiding sin and getting rid of our corrupt nature. It goes beyond simply undoing the effect of the Fall, as an old couplet shows:

In Christ the sons of Adam boast
More blessings than their father lost.

Our character should reflect the very image of Jesus Christ himself. God wants us to be "conformed to the image of his Son" (Rom 8:29). Paul writes elsewhere, "We all, with unveiled face, beholding the glory of the Lord, are being changed into his likeness from one degree of glory to another; for this comes from the Lord who is the Spirit" (2 Cor 3:18). Adam may have enjoyed many of God's blessings before he fell. But in his untried state he fell short of experiencing all that God ultimately intends for his people.

Virtue in the New Testament is always positive. We must not only avoid sin, but exercise the positive virtues in their place. Instead of yielding our members "to impurity and greater and greater iniquity," we are to yield our members to "righteousness for sanctification" (Rom 6:19). Paul brings this out very fully in his list of qualities in Ephesians 4:25-32. Notice that each sin is to be substituted by a positive virtue. Instead of lying, there is to be truth. Instead of stealing, there is to be work and generosity. Evil talk is to be replaced by what is edifying, while bitterness, wrath and anger are to be renounced in favor of kindness and forgiveness. To summarize in Paul's own way, we are not only to put off the old man but also to put on the new.

It is clear then that sanctification and holiness must result in good works. It is a matter of being "holy... in all your conduct" (1 Pet 1:15). In the language of our Lord, a sound tree produces good fruit just as a bad tree produces evil fruit (Mt 7:16-20). This is an essential result of abiding in Christ. Our Lord himself claimed, "He who abides in me, and I in him, he it is that bears much fruit" (Jn 15:5).

So sanctification is much more than a spiritual experience. Indeed, there can be a subtle piece of self-deception here. Experiences of "blessing" can be a substitute for practical holiness. Christians have sometimes claimed some great spiritual experience or attainment and yet remained just as selfish, bad tempered or undisciplined as before. Let us remember that the Holy Spirit produces fruit which includes the much needed virtues of "love, joy, peace, patience, kindness, goodness, faithfulness, gentleness, self-control" (Gal 5:22-23).

It would be a mistake, however, to imagine that holiness is just another word for moral improvement. If it were, holiness would be within the reach of an unregenerate person. Holiness is based on a relationship between the sinner and God, and the Christian seeks to be holy in order to please him and to glorify his name. Works of holiness spring out of the desire to obey God's will, in response to the Holy Spirit.

Holiness also includes another very positive factor which shows that it is much more than moral endeavor. Like the vessels in the Temple, we have been purified for a purpose, for, "if any one purifies himself from what is ignoble, then he will be a vessel for noble use, consecrated and useful to the master of the house, ready for any good work" (2 Tim 2:21). The same positive emphasis is made in the following verses on consecration: "I appeal to you therefore, brethren, by the mercies of God, to present your bodies as a living sacrifice, holy and acceptable to God, which is your spiritual worship. Do not be conformed to this world but be transformed by the renewal of your mind, that you may prove what is the will of God, what is good and acceptable and perfect" (Rom 12:1-2). We are reminded of the worship in the Temple. When our bodies are consecrated to God, like the animals sacrificed in Old Testament worship, they become the exclusive property of God, to be used for his service. Our minds too are consecrated, for they are to be renewed with the positive purpose of proving what is the will of God.

4
Sin

_____

If *we want an accurate view* of Christian holiness, then we had best begin with a long look at sin. So argued John Ryle in his volume of papers on holiness. He continued,

Wrong views about holiness are generally traceable to wrong views about human corruption. . . . If a man does not realize the dangerous nature of his soul's disease, you cannot wonder if he is content with false or imperfect remedies.[1]

Undoubtedly he was right. Shallow views about holiness and sanctification have nearly always been based on inadequate doctrines of sin. But the Bible gives a very serious diagnosis of the sin from which we need to be delivered. Nowhere does it play down its strength or the tenacity with which it clings to people. So we, too, ought to consider this topic before proceeding any further.

What Is Sin?

To this question we can give a simple and direct answer: any thought, word or deed is a sin if it is not in conformity with God's law. This is in accordance with the clear statement of Scripture that "sin is lawlessness" (1 Jn 3:4). Notice that God's law is the standard by which we are judged. Sin is not simply a failure to live according to our ability, but a failure to conform to God's revealed will and purpose. The world sometimes tells us to do our best, with the assurance that no one can do more. This may be so, but our best is still a long way short of God's commandment, and it is his standard which counts.

Here we have one of the supreme purposes of God's law: to reveal sin in its true character. In these days when it is fashionable to deprecate law as the basis for morality, it is especially important to consider it. When Paul asks, "Why then the law?" (i.e., in view of the gospel covenant with Abraham which the law cannot disannul), he answers, "It was added because of transgressions." The New English Bible surely brings out what was in the apostle's mind by rendering this last sentence, "It was added to make wrongdoing a legal offence" (Gal 3:19).

God's law, then, shows us that we are sinners. As Paul points out again and again in the Epistle to the Romans, "through the law comes knowledge of sin" (3:20), and "where there is no law there is no transgression" (4:15). (Compare also Romans 5:13 and 1 Timothy 1:8-11.) As Ernest F. Kevan pointed out:

> Legal concepts of sin are not on any account to be dismissed as artificial: rather are they the necessary expression of sin's heinousness and of the abhorrence with which God must view it. Law, therefore, does not give to

sin its awful, wrath-deserving nature: it merely provides a category in which to express this terrible fact.[2]

We must not forget that sin applies as much to the thought life as to words and deeds. We can commit adultery in the imagination (see Mt 5:27-28). Hatred is classed with murder, the only difference being that it is committed in the heart (1 Jn 3:15). This is not to say that the entry of an evil thought into the mind is in itself sinful. What is wrong is the entertaining of it. We have, of course, the well-known remark of Martin Luther that we cannot prevent the birds from flying over our heads, but we are responsible if the birds make nests in our hair! Indeed, we can break every one of the Ten Commandments in our thoughts. The way we occupy our minds is often the key to the way we speak and act. If we are victorious in the realm of the imagination, we conquer everywhere. If, on the other hand, we are defeated here, we fight a losing battle elsewhere. The way we think determines our character: "As he thinketh in his heart, so is he" (Prov 23:7 KJV). And, we might add, so does he.

In addition to this, sin extends beyond the wrong things we do to the things we ought to do but fail to do. To use the words of the General Confession in the Anglican Prayer Book, we sin when "we have left undone those things which we ought to have done" as much as when "we have done those things which we ought not to have done." It was for sins of omission that those "on the left hand" were judged in Christ's description of the Last Judgment (Mt 25:31-46). There is no mention of acts of sin, such as lying, cheating or murder. They were sent into everlasting fire because they had neglected to give food to the hungry, drink to the thirsty, clothing to the naked and so on.

This aspect of sin has frequently been forgotten by those who have made extravagant claims to sinless perfection. Even if they are innocent of all positive acts of sin (although this I find rather hard to believe!), can they honestly say they have always done all they could to relieve the needs of others? Over and above this, what about our duty toward God? Jesus sums up the first table of the law in the single command to love God with all our heart, soul and strength, and this he describes as "the first and great commandment." Who can honestly claim that he or she loves God in this wholehearted, single-minded way?

Some have tried to press a distinction between conscious and unconscious sin, holding that we can be all that God requires of us as long as we are free from conscious sin. Is this a biblical distinction? It is certainly not in accordance with the Old Testament, where we find Israel taught that sins committed unconsciously rendered people unclean and called for atonement. We find this clearly stated in Leviticus and also in Numbers (see, e.g., Lev 4; 5:14-19; Num 15:25-29). The psalmist expresses a constant concern when he prays, "Clear thou me from hidden faults" (Ps 19:12). And this is just as much the teaching of the New Testament as it is of the Old. Nowhere is anyone excused from sins because of ignorance. The servant "who did not know [the master's will], and did what deserved a beating" did not escape punishment (Lk 12:48). Again we quote Bishop Ryle: "We shall do well to remember, that when we make our own miserably imperfect knowledge and consciousness the measure of our sinfulness, we are on very dangerous ground."[3] Indeed, our very failure to discern sin is a sign that we are blind to moral issues and insensitive to what is wrong.

The Corruption of Human Nature
The origin of sins. Sins do not simply originate from our upbringing, although this does, of course, play a very important part. But our background cannot receive more than part of the blame. Our sins spring from a corrupt nature. It is a moral disease from which humanity is suffering, which has affected the very center of our being. "The heart is deceit-

ful above all things, and desperately corrupt" (Jer 17:9), and out of that heart springs all our wrongdoing.

Our Lord drew attention to this unpleasant moral fact when he was showing the inadequacy of external ritual cleansings. He pointed out that things from outside do not defile a person, but rather what comes out of his or her own inner nature:

What comes out of a man is what defiles a man. For from within, out of the heart of man, come evil thoughts, fornication, theft, murder, adultery, coveting, wickedness, deceit, licentiousness, envy, slander, pride, foolishness. All these evil things come from within, and they defile a man. (Mk 7:20-23)

Elsewhere, in Luke 6, Jesus compares a person to a tree. Just as diseased fruit indicates corruption in the tree itself, so "an evil man out of the evil treasure of his heart bringeth forth that which is evil: for of the abundance of the heart his mouth speaketh" (v. 45 KJV). All this means that as long as the heart is diseased by sin it has a continual propensity to evil, which can make itself shown sometimes at a very early age. As the psalmist observed, "The wicked go astray from the womb, they err from their birth, speaking lies" (Ps 58:3). Indeed, a person can be described as a rebel from birth (Is 48:8).

Erroneous views of sin. Here is a point at which some views of sin are hopelessly unrealistic and inadequate. Some have refused to recognize as sin anything but external acts, a view from which the Church of England has officially dissociated itself in its Articles:

Original sin standeth not in the following of Adam, (as the Pelagians do vainly talk;) but it is the fault and corruption of the Nature of every man, that naturally is engendered of the offspring of Adam; whereby man is very far gone from original righteousness, and is of his own nature inclined to evil, so that the flesh lusteth always contrary to the Spirit. (Article 9)

This shallow view of sin was one of the errors of the Pharisees of our Lord's day. It led to their overemphasis of external rituals and cleansings criticized by Jesus in Mark 7. This externalizing of sin can involve a person in the subtle error of, to use James Philip's words, "exchanging one set of sins for another, and mistaking this for deliverance." He continues:

> It is a supreme tragedy—and very frightening—when a man, under the impression that he is being saved from sin, merely alters the pattern of sin in his life, from the less respectable and more obvious, to the less obvious and more respectable. The evil one is well satisfied to bring about such a deception.[4]

The story of the Pharisee and the publican is a good illustration of this all-too-common mistake. James Philip again goes straight to the heart of the story:

> The real force of the parable lies in the exposure of the complete self-centredness of [the Pharisee's] life, religious though it was. It is his self-consciousness and self-absorption that obtrude throughout. The real problem of his life had never been touched; self was deeply entrenched and reigning supreme.[5]

Not a benign growth. Many people, however, are willing to recognize that sin is basically an inward principle working contrary to God's will and inclining the person to evil, yet they have tried to localize it. They have spoken of a person's sinful nature as something which can be readily isolated and, if necessary, eradicated. For such people the work of sanctification is a comparatively simple affair. A sinful nature can be extracted like a bad tooth—and some views of sinless perfection have virtually amounted to this. However, our condition cannot be so simply cured. Sin is not like a demon residing somewhere within us that can be thrown out in one piece. It is far more accurately described (again in the words of Article 9) as an "infection of nature"; and it is an infection that "doth remain, yea in them that are regenerated." The Westminster

Confession of Presbyterian churches uses similar language, reproduced almost word for word by the Baptist Confession of 1689.

Unfortunately, our sinful nature is not like a benign growth which can be removed by a surgeon. The words of the General Confession, "there is no health in us," expose the seriousness of our condition. The whole of our being has been saturated with the poison, and the remedy is better seen in terms of medicine than of surgery. There is therefore no quick cure, no short cut to sanctification. It is "that the sinful body (KJV, "whole body of sin") might be destroyed, and we might no longer be enslaved to sin" (Rom 6:6). God does not only have to deal with what we do, or with what we contain, but with what we are.

Let us try to avoid misunderstanding here. We are not saying that everyone is as bad as could be. Even unregenerate people are capable of noble acts. What we must emphasize is that every part of us is to some degree infected. Nothing we do is perfect because all our actions are tainted; judged by God's standards, even "all our righteous deeds are like a polluted garment" (Is 64:6). Sin is like a drop of ink in a glass of water. It is diffused throughout the glass. The water may be only slightly blue, but nonetheless the entire contents of the glass are colored to some degree.

Our Twofold Need
Because of sin, we have a double need which is fully met by what God has done for us in Christ: a need arising first from the guilt of sin and then from its pollution.

As we have seen, sin is the transgression of God's law. By that law humanity is judged and found guilty. As a result, we are under God's condemnation and the object of his wrath. The penalty for infringing God's law is death, not only physical but also spiritual and eternal; "the wages of sin is death" (Rom 6:23). And so God's law is also called "the law of sin and death" (Rom 8:2). While we are in this position before God, not only is there no hope for us in eternity, but there is equally no possibility of gaining the victory over the sinful nature for which we are condemned.

We therefore need to be restored to favor with God. We need to be pronounced "Not Guilty" so that we can have dealings with the God we so desperately need. In other words, we need to be "justified." It is this very thing that God has done for us through the death of Jesus Christ. To describe it in Paul's words: "Therefore, since we are justified by faith, we have peace with God through our Lord Jesus Christ" (Rom 5:1). And by this very fact, "There is therefore now no condemnation for those who are in Christ Jesus.... The law of the Spirit of life in Christ Jesus has set [us] free from the law of sin and death" (Rom 8:1-2).

But sin has done far more than impair our relationship with God. It has also polluted our nature so that we are not only guilty in God's sight and condemned, but also defiled and corrupt. It is as much the purpose of God to save us from this defilement as it is to remove our guilt. God does not justify a person so that he or she can continue in sin with impunity. "By no means! How can we who died to sin still live in it?" (Rom 6:2). God does not save us in sin, but from sin. The work of sanctification is concerned with this aspect of salvation. The Holy Spirit takes a sinner and sets him apart from sin and for God, so that instead of serving sin he serves God. Not only is there a change in the person's standing before God, but also a change in his or her inward condition. The sin which had infected and corrupted will have to be subdued, weakened and removed. David confessed to this need when he prayed, "Create in me a clean heart, O God, and put a new and right spirit within me" (Ps 51:10).

Here is where sanctification comes in. The Spirit works to purify and cleanse the heart and life of the believer until ultimately he or she perfectly reflects the very character of

Christ himself. It is important, however, to distinguish sanctification from justification, because confusing the two has often caused considerable error. In the next two chapters we shall consider sanctification and how it is achieved. We shall then be in a position to see more clearly how this doctrine differs from justification.

5
The
Means of
Sanctification

From *beginning to end* sanctification is the work of God. Nobody ever made himself or herself holy, for holiness is far beyond the reach of the natural person. The apostle Paul points this out impressively. After working through a list of obligations which he lays upon his readers, he says, "May the God of peace himself sanctify you wholly" (1 Thess 5:23). Paul acknowledges that although he can exhort and command his readers and place before them the motives for obedience, only God can sanctify them and so enable them to obey.

Its Distinction from Moral Virtue
Sanctification is then, in the words of the Westminster Cate-

chism, "the work of God's free grace." This is another of the ways in which scriptural holiness is quite different from mere moral virtue. John Owen extols such moral virtue and says it

> is the best thing among men, that is of themselves. It far exceeds in worth, use and satisfaction, all that the honours, powers, profits, and pleasures of the world can extend unto . . . and very eminent instances of the practice of it were given in the lives of some of them, whose examples of righteousness, temperance, and equanimity in all conditions, now rise up to the shame of many called Christians, and will be called over at the last day, as an aggravation of their condemnation.

However, having said all this, Owen goes on, "But to suppose that this moral virtue, however excellent, is that holiness of truth which believers receive by the spirit of Christ, is to debase and overthrow it, and to drive men from seeking an interest in it.[1]

We must never lose sight of this important emphasis. There is a subtle danger of speaking of sanctification as essentially coming from our own effort or initiative. We can unconsciously do this even while acknowledging our need for the power of the Holy Spirit, by making the operation of that power dependent upon our surrender and consecration. Sometimes the work of the Holy Spirit is virtually depersonalized, and "Holy Ghost power" ("an objectionable phrase," comments B. B. Warfield) is said to be at our disposal. Warfield continues thus:

> God stands always helplessly by until man calls Him into action by opening a channel into which His energies may flow. It sounds dreadfully like turning on the steam or the electricity. This representation is employed not only with reference to the great matters of salvation and sanctification, in which God's operations are "secured" (or released) by our faith, but also with reference to every blessing be-

stowed by Him. We are not only constantly exhorted to "claim" blessings, but the enjoyment of these blessings is with wearying iteration suspended on our "claiming" them. It is expressly declared that God cannot bless us in any way until we open the way for His action by an act of our own will. Everywhere and always the initiative belongs to man; everywhere and always God's action is suspended upon man's will. . . . . It is nothing less than degrading to God to suppose Him thus subject to the control of man and unable to move except as man permits Him to do so, or to produce any effects except as He is turned into the channels of their working at man's option.[2]

God's Activity, Not Ours

Sanctification, in Scripture, is always something which God does. It is he who takes us, sets us apart and then refines our nature and challenges us to live accordingly. "Man does not 'secure' the grace of God: the grace of God 'secures' the activities of man."[3] What we intend to do now is to study the way God sanctifies his people and, especially, the agents he employs.

Some years ago I received considerable help from a book by Harry Ironside, *Holiness: The False and the True*, which has unfortunately long been out of print. Ironside names three agents of sanctification which we will now examine: the blood of Christ, the Holy Spirit and the Word of God.

Sanctification by the Blood of Christ: Eternal

The Epistle to the Hebrews teaches that Christ's sacrificial death sanctifies the believer for all time, as the following quotations demonstrate:

> For if the sprinkling of defiled persons with the blood of goats and bulls and with the ashes of a heifer sanctifies for the purification of the flesh, how much more shall the blood of Christ, who through the eternal Spirit offered

himself without blemish to God, purify your conscience from dead works to serve the living God. (9:13-14)

By that will we have been sanctified through the offering of the body of Jesus Christ once for all. (10:10)

For by a single offering he has perfected for all time those who are sanctified. (10:14)

How much worse punishment do you think will be deserved by the man who has spurned the Son of God, and profaned the blood of the covenant by which he was sanctified, and outraged the Spirit of grace? (10:29)

So Jesus also suffered outside the gate in order to sanctify the people through his own blood. (13:12)

An examination of these verses leads to several observations. First, we are looking at not an internal work of the Holy Spirit, but rather the basis on which a Christian is set apart by God. Because of Christ's death, Christians may regard themselves as on the Godward side of the gulf which separates God from human sin. Because they have been cleansed from sin and their consciences purged, Christians are entitled to forget their past sins. They are brought into a lasting and intimate relationship with Jesus Christ, for "he who sanctifies and those who are sanctified have all one origin. That is why he is not ashamed to call them brethren" (Heb 2:11). The word often used to describe this aspect of sanctification is *positional*.

Second, sanctification is an accomplished fact that depends on the sufficiency of the one offering of Jesus Christ at Calvary. This is why Paul can address the Corinthian Christians as "saints." They had not attained any high level of sanctification in practice, but they had been set apart to God by virtue of Christ's death and were "sanctified in Christ Jesus" (1 Cor 1:1-2 and also 1:30). Sanctification, in these terms, is certainly no experience or process subsequent to conversion. Indeed, if a Christian is asked when he was sanctified, in the sense that the Epistle to the Hebrews uses this word, the answer is not to be found in his experience at all. There is only one possible answer to such a question: "I was sanctified two thousand years ago at Calvary!" Our sanctification was accomplished then and stands eternally complete (Heb 10:14).

It is possible for a person to have this status by outward association with the people of God without necessarily enjoying its inward reality. The New Testament finds an example of this in the children of Israel in the wilderness. In spite of all their outward privileges, they failed to enter the promised land because of unbelief. Here is a solemn warning for us (see, e.g., Heb 3—4 and compare 1 Cor 10). Hebrews 10:26-29 shows that a person can even have the privilege of sanctification as an outward status and yet be eternally lost.

This last point, incidentally, throws light on Paul's reference to the children of a believer, and even the unbelieving husband or wife, as "holy" (1 Cor 7:14). By family relationship such a person has become outwardly associated with God's people and is therefore "sanctified by the wife" or "sanctified by the husband." Because of this a Christian was to continue to live with an unbelieving partner instead of forsaking him or her and the children. Otherwise it might have seemed that the holiness of a Christian demanded separation from an unbelieving partner. Paul even sees this as an encouragement to look for the conversion of the non-Christian husband or wife.[4]

Sanctification by the Holy Spirit: Internal

Biblical theology has always recognized that sanctification has much to do with the Holy Spirit. When holiness is ascribed to God in the New Testament (except where the Old Testament is being quoted), it is nearly always ascribed to the third person of the Trinity. He is referred to as "the Holy Spirit" more than a hundred times. This is hardly surprising, for it is the Holy Spirit's function to make the Christian's eternal status an inward reality. He takes the benefits of what Jesus Christ has done on the cross and applies them to the individual believer's heart.

To be accurate here, we will restrict ourselves to verses in the New Testament which use the actual word *sanctify* and attribute this work to the Holy Spirit. In 1 Corinthians 6 Paul gives a list of sins which many of his readers in their pre-Christian days had been guilty of. But he then goes on to show the difference the gospel has made to them: "And such were some of you. But you were washed, you were sanctified, you were justified in the name of the Lord Jesus and in the Spirit of our God" (v. 11). We see here that the change they had experienced, including this sanctification, is attributed to the Spirit of God and all that is signified by "the name of the Lord Jesus."

A second reference shows the close relationship of the sanctifying work of the Holy Spirit with other basic doctrines: "To the exiles, ... chosen and destined by God the Father and sanctified by the Spirit for obedience to Jesus Christ and for sprinkling with his blood: May grace and peace be multiplied to you" (1 Pet 1:1-2). Again we see that God's electing purposes are effected by the sanctifying work of the Holy Spirit; but notice the significant addition, "for obedience to Jesus Christ and for sprinkling with his blood." In other words, the intended result of a person being set apart by God's Holy Spirit is that he or she should be obedient and receive the benefits of the shed blood of Jesus Christ. As Alan M. Stibbs comments, "The end in view is *obedience*—that the elect should serve the divine pleasure. Participation in such a destiny requires also the *sprinkling of the blood of Jesus Christ.*"[5] The sanctifying work of the Holy Spirit is thus fundamental to our salvation: by means of it we share in the blessings of Christ's death.

In Romans 15:16 sanctification is again directly attributed to the Holy Spirit. Paul speaks of the grace given him by God "to be a minister of Christ Jesus to the Gentiles in the priestly service of the gospel of God, so that the offering of the Gentiles may be acceptable, sanctified by the Holy Spirit." Here the apostle sees his preaching of the gospel to the Gentiles in terms of offering them up as a sacrifice to God. Yet he recognizes that they could be acceptable to God only as the Holy Spirit sanctified them. Robert Haldane remarks, "As the sacrifices under the law were sanctified externally and typically, this figurative sacrifice is sanctified truly by the Holy Ghost. No person, then, can be acceptable to God who is not sanctified by His Spirit."[6] It is clear from these verses that sanctification by the Holy Spirit is closely connected with a person's conversion and is fundamental to his or her entire experience of Christ. It has to do with the very beginning of God's work in a person's life. It marks the moment when the Holy Spirit makes the believer's eternal status through Christ's death an inward reality.

It is easy to see now why Christians in the New Testament are so often described as "the saints in Christ Jesus." We can also see why Christians are spoken of as "those who are sanctified." In the Greek this is a perfect participle, which means that a Christian's sanctification is to be regarded as an accomplished fact (see Acts 20:32; 26:18; 1 Cor 1:2).

This gives us a second possible answer to the question "When were you sanctified?" "I was sanctified by the Holy Spirit when he opened my eyes to the truth, convicted me of my need and brought me to the shed blood of Jesus Christ." Incidentally this demonstrates how inappropriate it is to apply the word *sanctification* to any experience following conversion. As Harry Ironside summarizes these findings, "Far from being 'the second blessing,' subsequent to justification, it is a work apart from which none ever would be saved."[7]

Sanctification by the Word of God: External Results
The Holy Spirit's work in us goes beyond setting us apart for

the service of God and bringing us into a relationship with Jesus Christ. His intention is to mold our lives to the likeness of Christ himself. So in 1 Peter 1 those who have already been addressed as "chosen... and sanctified by the Spirit" are enjoined to be holy. Here is how Peter puts it: "But as he who called you is holy, be holy yourselves in all your conduct; since it is written, 'You shall be holy, for I am holy' " (1 Pet 1:15-16). In other words, our eternal status which has been made inwardly real by the Holy Spirit of God now has to be worked out in terms of everyday living—"in all your conduct." Paul was saying much the same when he told the Philippians, "Work out your own salvation with fear and trembling; for God is at work in you, both to will and to work for his good pleasure" (Phil 2:12-13). To put it briefly, "Work out what God has worked in." Because God is working in their hearts by his Holy Spirit, Paul can expect them to go on living the Christian life even in his absence.

A pattern for Christian living.   How then do we put sanctification to practical effect? Do we just leave it passively to the Holy Spirit and find ourselves doing naturally what we should? Is it simply a matter of "Love, and do as you wish"? Augustine's words are only partially true when we apply them to the matter of practical sanctification. In his Word, God has given us a pattern for Christian living. No Christian who wants to live a life of practical holiness can afford to ignore it. So we have the question which the psalmist both asks and answers (Ps 119:9): "How can a young man keep his way pure? By guarding it according to thy word." If the Word of God is to have the effect intended, it must be diligently obeyed. Here we need the practical teaching which we find in the Epistles.

The third agent of sanctification, then, is the Word of God which teaches us not only about the blood of Christ and the work of the Holy Spirit, but also about how God expects his provision to work out in practice. As Berkhof sees it, "Scripture presents all the objective conditions for holy exercises and acts. It serves to excite spiritual activity by presenting motives and inducements, and gives direction to it by prohibitions, exhortations, and examples, I Pet 1:22; 2:2; II Pet 1:4."[8] Christ himself recognizes the part played by the Word of God in our sanctification when he prays for his disciples, "Sanctify them in the truth; thy word is truth" (Jn 17:17). Jesus had already drawn attention to the cleansing effect of his Word an hour or two earlier when he had been with his disciples in the upper room: "You are already made clean by the word which I have spoken to you" (Jn 15:3).

But holiness is no mere negative concept simply involving avoidance of sin, for a holy life is one which is unreservedly devoted to the service of God. The Word of God gives essential direction for this life. It is by the Scriptures "that the man of God may be complete, equipped for every good work" (2 Tim 3:17). Charles Kingsley Barrett says that the truth which is God's Word "designates and separates the apostles for their mission."[9]

A pattern for the heart. The Scriptures should have an effect on the inner life of the believer as well as on his or her overt behavior. Jeremiah foresaw this striking feature of the new covenant: "This is the covenant which I will make with the house of Israel after those days, says the LORD: I will put my law within them, and I will write it upon their hearts" (Jer 31:33). Paul speaks in these terms when he is writing to the Corinthians. He describes his readers as "a letter from Christ delivered by us, written not with ink but with the Spirit of the living God, not in tablets of stone but on tablets of human hearts" (2 Cor 3:3). The apostle sees the Word he has been ministering written in the very hearts of the Corinthians, and the Holy Spirit is the ink with which he has been writing. The Corinthians have become letters of commendation for his ministry. The writer of Psalm 119 anticipated the same when he declared, "I have laid up thy word in my heart, that

I might not sin against thee" (Ps 119:11).

We have to recognize that our mind (or "conscience" as we call it when dealing with moral issues) is not sufficient of itself to guide us. O. Hallesby has compared the conscience to a court of law. The latter has judicial but not legislative authority. It is not for a court to make laws or to express any opinions about existing laws, but to apply them to the situation in hand. So it is for a Christian. A Christian's conscience is not at liberty to decide general principles of right and wrong, but to apply them in given situations. Clearly, then, the conscience is reliable only if it is under the law of God.

We must not lose sight of the importance of God's law for our sanctification, especially as many today deprecate it as the basis of Christian morality. Admittedly, the law by itself is insufficient to secure a life of practical holiness. Indeed, no part of God's Word has any effect apart from the Holy Spirit, and this is clearly recognized in Scripture. However, we are thinking here of the person who has been set apart by the Holy Spirit and who is willing to live in fellowship with the Spirit. And it is possible for such a person to fulfill God's law. Here is how Paul puts it: "In order that the just requirement of the law might be fulfilled in us, who walk not according to the flesh but according to the Spirit" (Rom 8:4). We shall return to this in chapter thirteen. For the moment let us unite God's law with his Spirit, and recognize that the Holy Spirit's purpose is to produce in the Christian all that the law demands.

It would be wrong, however, to imagine that the only part God's Word plays in our sanctification is in issuing commands. We are also encouraged to claim many promises in God's Word. Both aspects of God's Word appear in these lines from William Cowper's hymn:

Precepts and promises afford
    A sanctifying light.

In 2 Corinthians 7:1 Paul himself uses the promises of God as an incentive to practical sanctification: "Since we have these promises, beloved, let us cleanse ourselves from every defilement of the body and spirit, and make holiness perfect in the fear of God." On this ground Christians are called upon to live a separated life, forsaking anything which would tarnish or mar their testimony.

This brings us to a third answer to our question "When were you sanctified?" In addition to pointing to the death of Christ on the cross and the moment when we ourselves were brought to a knowledge of him, we can say that we are being sanctified day by day as we apply the teachings of God's Word to our lives. The practical conclusion is obvious. If anyone would live a life of holiness, the study of the Bible is indispensable. We need to read it with both a short-term and a long-term policy. Our immediate aim will be to obey it promptly, for we are to be "doers of the word, and not hearers only" (Jas 1:22). At the same time our aim will also be a long-term one, for the man or woman in whom the Holy Spirit truly dwells and whose mind is constantly being filled with the Word of God is bound to find his or her whole outlook and attitude toward life gradually being changed. We will then say with Luther, "My conscience is captive to the Word of God."

6
Progressive Sanctification —Renewal

We saw in the previous chapter that our sanctification works itself out progressively. The Shorter Catechism, defining sanctification, uses the word *renewal:* "Sanctification is the work of God's free grace, whereby we are renewed in the whole man after the image of God, and are enabled more and more to die unto sin, and live unto righteousness." In this chapter we shall examine the use and meaning of this word in Scripture. The Greek word itself means "making new again," that is, restoring something to what was originally intended before it aged or became spoiled. This is what God does when he sanctifies a life which has been marred by sin. There is, however, another doctrine which ought to be considered first so that we can see the idea of renewal in its right context.

Renewal Begins with Regeneration

Sanctification has to do with the deep injury which sin has done to the lives of people—with corruption and pollution. This involves spiritual death; people by nature are "dead through... trespasses and sins" (Eph 2:1), and their minds have been blinded by the "god of this world" (see 2 Cor 4:4). In short, we need to be renewed. Now the initial stage, fundamental to the whole process of renewal, is regeneration, or new birth. Jesus told Nicodemus: "Unless one is born anew, he cannot see the kingdom of God" (Jn 3:3). Once, however, God has made that one alive (Eph 2:5; Jn 5:21) and shone the light of truth into his or her heart (2 Cor 4:6), then the work of renewal has begun.

Titus 3:5 implies that the Holy Spirit begins renewing people right after their regeneration: "He saved us, not because of deeds done by us in righteousness, but in virtue of his own mercy, by the washing of regeneration and renewal in the Holy Spirit."[1] The Prayer Book Collect for Christmas Day expresses it well: "Grant that we being regenerate ... may daily be renewed by Thy Holy Spirit." This is a prayer for renewal based on the assumption of regeneration. Renewal cannot begin until a person has been born again of God's Spirit.

Some Remarks about Renewal

The following verses will serve as a basis for some further observations:

He saved us... by the washing of regeneration and renewal in the Holy Spirit. (Tit 3:5)

Do not be conformed to this world but be transformed by the renewal of your mind. (Rom 12:2)

Though our outer nature is wasting away, our inner nature is being renewed every day. (2 Cor 4:16)

[You] have put on the new nature, which is being renewed... after the image of its creator. (Col 3:10)

Be renewed in the spirit of your minds. (Eph 4:23)

A work of the Holy Spirit. The first of the above verses makes it clear that it is the Holy Spirit who renews us. We do not do it by our own effort. This is in keeping with the constant teaching of the Bible. It is the Holy Spirit's work to subdue the desires of the flesh (Gal 5:16-24), to promote holiness and so on. Christian virtues are referred to as "the fruit of the Spirit" (Gal 5:22-23; compare Eph 5:9). We "worship God in the spirit" (Phil 3:3 KJV). We love God's people "in the Spirit" (Col 1:8), and we purify our souls "in obeying the truth through the Spirit" (1 Pet 1:22 KJV). Lying behind every exertion of the Christian to work out his or her salvation is the Holy Spirit's work "to will and to work for his good pleasure" (Phil 2:13). "To will" points to the Spirit's work of creating in us the desire and intention to work out our salvation. "To work" speaks of his work in enabling us to put this desire into effect—or to translate the Greek word literally, "energizing" it.

An inward work. The human mind needs to be renewed, as Holy Scripture has consistently emphasized. For example, the Lord said of the Israelites in the wilderness: "Oh that they had such a mind as this always, to fear me and to keep all my commandments" (Deut 5:29). This inward work of the Holy Spirit was foretold through the prophet Ezekiel when God said, "And I will give them one heart, and put a new spirit within them; I will take the stony heart out of their flesh and give them a heart of flesh" (Ezek 11:19). That is, in place of inward deadness God intended to give life. So renewal is not just a matter of copying an outward pattern, although it may well include that, but is something far deeper. "Let this mind be in you, which was also in Christ Jesus" (Phil 2:5 KJV), Paul urges. And for a God who "desirest truth in the inward being" (Ps 51:6) nothing less than this will do.

But sanctification involves more than keeping a sinful nature in check. While it includes outward victory and count-

eracting the insinuations of our fallen nature, it is far more.
Renewal affects the spirit, soul and body (1 Thess 5:23). It
is as unbiblical to suppose that our sinful nature should remain unchanged throughout life as to believe that it can be
totally eradicated.[2] We may well pray:

O Thou Spirit divine
All my nature refine,
Till the beauty of Jesus
    Be seen in me.

This makes another difference between sanctification and
moral reformation. To show social graces and be nicely man-
nered is no proof of inward renewal. To use the simile of
Charles Hodge, "The two things differ in nature as much as
a clean heart from clean clothes." Sanctification is not to be
confused with moral training: "Such training is not to be
undervalued. It is enjoined in the Word of God. It cannot,
however, change the nature. It cannot impart life. A faultless
statue fashioned out of pure marble in all its beauty, is far
below a living man."[3]

A process. The quotations from both Corinthians and Colossians use a present passive to express the work of renewal,
and this implies that it is a present process, that the inner
person "is being renewed." At this point it is worth quot-
ing a verse where the cognate adjective *kainos* is employed:
"If any one is in Christ, he is a new creation; the old has
passed away, behold, the new has come" (2 Cor 5:17; cf
Gal 6:15). A Christian, we are told here, is a new creation,
but from what we have seen it is clear that this creation is by
no means complete. It is therefore appropriate to pray, in the
words of Charles Wesley's hymn,

Finish then Thy new creation:
    Pure and spotless let us be.

Paul brings out a thrilling aspect of this process when he
contrasts it with what is happening in the body. "Though
our outer nature is wasting away, our inner nature is being

renewed every day" (2 Cor 4:16). The spiritual process is a complete reversal of its bodily counterpart. Our bodies begin with the health and vigor of youth and then gradually decline to the weakness of old age and, ultimately, death. Our spiritual history is the complete opposite. Instead of a healthy and vigorous nature, a Christian begins with a nature corrupted and weakened by sin. From this unpromising start the believer is daily renewed by the Holy Spirit and can look forward to the day when this sanctifying process will be complete. It is because of the certainty of the Spirit's work that the apostle is able to say, "We do not lose heart" (2 Cor 4:16).

Requiring active obedience. Although renewal is a work of the Holy Spirit, the subject is always active rather than passive. We have to work out our salvation. We hear this when Paul writes, "Put on the new nature": renewal involves active obedience to God's will.

In Ephesians 4:23 renewal is commanded. Colossians 3:10, on the other hand, confirms that the readers did take the first steps toward renewal. These verses stress God's part and ours in the work of renewal. The apostle makes it quite clear that the new nature is not produced by the person but is rather "created after the likeness of God in true righteousness and holiness" (Eph 4:24). The same point is made in the Epistle to the Colossians, where Paul speaks of the "new nature, which is being renewed in knowledge after the image of its creator" (Col 3:10). But while this new nature is created and renewed by God, Paul insists that it has to be put on, just as the old life has to be put off.

So we know that a person's own part in sanctification is not independent of the Holy Spirit. We are not to imagine that sanctification is partly God's work and partly ours. There is no division of labor, as if God had said, "You do your part and I will do mine." Rather, our moral exertions and the diligence with which we use the means of grace—such as Bible study, prayer and fellowship with other Christians—result from God's work within us. There is no denial of our own efforts when we sing of the Holy Spirit,

And every virtue we possess,
And every victory won,
And every thought of holiness,
Are his alone.

The call to sanctification is often issued as a command. Where the Spirit of God is renewing a person, he challenges that one to action. Take, for example, his call to the people of Isaiah's day to cleanse themselves from all sinful and doubtful things and to devote themselves to good works: "Wash yourselves; make yourselves clean; remove the evil of your doings from before my eyes; cease to do evil; learn to do good; seek justice, correct oppression; defend the fatherless, plead for the widow" (Is 1:16-17). Jeremiah makes a similar command: "O Jerusalem, wash your heart from wickedness" (Jer 4:14). Again, in the verse quoted earlier Paul demands, "Since we have these promises . . . let us cleanse ourselves from every defilement of body and spirit" (2 Cor 7:1).

The way to cleanse our conduct, according to Psalm 119:9, is "by *guarding it* according to thy word." Fighting against the devil's temptations, we shall need to remember James's word: "Resist the devil and he will flee from you" (Jas 4:7). To summarize in the words of John Owen, "God works in us and with us, not against us or without us; so that His assistance is an encouragement as to the facilitating of the work, and no occasion of neglect as to the work itself."[4]

This, of course, is one of the ways in which renewal differs from regeneration. In regeneration we are passive. We can no more help ourselves than a baby can help in its own birth. But in our renewal, we are fellow workers with God.

That renewal is a process we have already observed. Paul in Colossians applies this process to the new nature which is ours in Christ and adds a further feature—the goal in view.

Paul describes this goal as the image of its creator.

We know that God created the first Adam in his own image (Gen 1:26-27) and that this image was impaired by the Fall. It is God's purpose in Christ now to restore this image so that we may "share in his holiness" (Heb 12:10). At regeneration a Christian is born into God's family, and as he or she subsequently grows up one may expect certain family characteristics to appear. Christ may be regarded as the elder brother who displays to perfection how the character of God may be expressed in a human life. So the goal of renewal is "to be conformed to the image of his Son, in order that he might be the first-born among many brethren" (Rom 8:29).

7
Sanctification and Justification

W_e now come to the_ all-important matter of distinguishing between sanctification and justification. We have already seen in chapter four that these two doctrines correspond to the two main effects of sin. Justification deals with our condemnation in God's sight, while sanctification is his answer to our sinful condition. Having studied the biblical usage of _sanctify_ and _renew_, we are now in a position to pursue the relationship between justification and sanctification. We will begin with a brief summary of the doctrine of justification, and then go on to see where sanctification differs from it.

The Meaning of Justification
The word _justification_ is basically a legal term. This is already

apparent from our introduction to it at the end of chapter four. It becomes still more apparent in the following quotation, which is fairly typical of the word's use in Scripture: "If there is a dispute between men, ... the judges decide between them, acquitting [KJV, justifying] the innocent and condemning the wicked" (Deut 25:1). From this verse it is clear that justifying people does not affect their moral condition. When a judge declares someone "Not Guilty," the judge is simply giving that person a legal standing. The same applies in legal practice today. When a jury gives a verdict of "Not Guilty," it is not reforming the prisoner. Rather, on the basis of the evidence which they have been considering, the jurors declare that in the eyes of the law the person is to be treated as not guilty; as a result the judge acquits the prisoner. Deuteronomy 25:1 also shows that "justify" is the opposite of "condemn." This is plain, too, from Jesus' statement: "By your words you will be justified, and by your words you will be condemned" (Mt 12:37).

What happens to a sinner when he or she stands before the God who is "the Judge of all the earth" (Gen 18:25)? The Bible has only one answer: the sinner is condemned. Judged by the standards of God's law, everyone has come hopelessly short. Everyone has broken the great and first commandment (Mt 22:38) by failing to give God the place in life which is his due. Of course, most of us at some time try to excuse ourselves and pretend that we are quite good enough because we manage to appear respectable before the eyes of our fellow human beings. All this, however, is useless before God. He has before him all the evidence, including the true condition of our hearts. Jesus said to the Pharisees, "You are those who justify yourselves before men, but God knows your hearts" (Lk 16:15). If we face the true facts of God's law, we are forced to confess with the psalmist, "Enter not into judgment with thy servant; for no man living is righteous before thee" (Ps 143:2).

How then can a sinner be justified (declared righteous) by a holy and righteous God? How is one to attain the legal standing of "Not Guilty" in the sight of such a judge? In human law there is only one way for a guilty person to be justified, and that is by the sentence which the law requires being carried out. Once this has been completed, then the law's requirements have been satisfied and, as far as the law is concerned, the offender is free of his guilt. But this is no answer to the problem of a sinner found guilty before God, for "the wages of sin is death" (Rom 6:23): physical and spiritual, eternal and final.

Yet God in his grace and mercy has made it possible for sinners to be declared righteous before him.

They are justified by his grace as a gift, through the redemption which is in Christ Jesus, whom God put forward as an expiation [KJV, propitiation] by his blood, to be received by faith. This was to show God's righteousness, because in his divine forbearance he had passed over former sins. (Rom 3:24-25)

When Christ shed his blood on the cross, he died the death which was our due, in our place and on our behalf. "It was to prove at the present time that he himself is righteous and that he justifies him who has faith in Jesus" (Rom 3:26). As a result, "there is therefore now no condemnation for those who are in Christ Jesus" (Rom 8:1), and so, on the ground of what Jesus Christ has done on the cross, God can pronounce the sinner who believes in Christ "Not Guilty," "Uncondemned," "Justified."

Sanctification Differs

If we compare this brief description of justification with the biblical teaching on sanctification, striking differences emerge. The former is legal, external and objective, while sanctification, relating to the purifying of heart and life, is experiential, internal and subjective. Instead of being concerned with our outward standing, sanctification applies to our inward condition.[1]

And there is another difference. A person is justified by a sovereign, once-for-all declaration of God the Father, just as a court of law makes a similar declaration concerning a defendant. Sanctification, however, is a gradual process which is effected by the inner working of the Holy Spirit. The process begins when the Holy Spirit first sets a sinner apart and imparts new life by the act of regeneration. It continues in the inward renewal of his nature. It is not completed until the end of this present life when he is glorified and made like Christ. We shall consider this final stage of sanctification, usually called "glorification," in chapter fifteen.

Failure to distinguish between justification and sanctification has been one of the errors of the Roman Catholic Church. It assumes that justification has to do with being *made* (as distinct from being *declared*) righteous. No doubt the Latin language has helped to create this confusion, for *justificio*, from which the English word *justify* is derived, was an unfortunate way to translate the Hebrew and Greek word we have been studying. This Latin word does in fact mean literally "to make righteous," which, as we have seen, is not the meaning of the Hebrew and Greek of Scripture.

The Roman Catholic Church has made many attempts to discover its doctrine in Scripture. In a fairly recent textbook of Roman Catholic teaching, Ludwig Ott claims that justification is a true eradication of sin; he further explains: "Holy Writ conceives the forgiveness of sins as a real and complete removal of the sins."[2] This is tantamount to saying that it is sanctification. He then attempts to uphold this statement with a list of Bible expressions, complete with biblical references, but it is noticeable that the word *justify* is strangely missing from all his examples! For his statement that "Scripture represents justification... as a sanctification," he quotes 1 Corinthians 6:11![3]

Different mode of appropriation. Both of these doctrines demand of us a response, and one of the very important differences between the two is the nature of that response. Notice first of all that both justification and sanctification are secured by faith. Justification by faith is one of the cardinal doctrines in Scripture: it is when a person believes in Christ that God declares him or her righteous. The Epistle to the Romans in particular emphasizes this.[4] Faith is also essential to sanctification, and in Acts we have the very expression "sanctified by faith" (26:18). So when the apostle told the Philippian jailer, "Believe in the Lord Jesus, and you will be saved" (Acts 16:31), we have every reason to believe that Paul had in mind salvation in all its aspects, including sanctification.

The two differ, however, over the place given to works and effort. In justification these have no place at all. This was what Luther meant by *per fidem solam*, "by faith alone." We can do nothing to earn or merit our justification, for no matter how hard we try we still fall short of the moral standards that God has revealed in his law. Paul underscores this when he says, "For by grace you have been saved through faith; and this is not your own doing, it is the gift of God—not because of works, lest any man should boast" (Eph 2:8-9). Paul uses here for his verb form the perfect participle, which could render the translation "By grace are you *in a position of having been saved* through faith." So he refers to the Christians' justification as a past, accomplished fact, in contrast to their sanctification, which is essentially a present process.

This is a further point of difference with the Roman Catholic Church. Canon 24 of the Council of Trent states:

If anyone saith, that the justice received is not preserved and also increased before God through good works; but that the said works are merely the fruits and signs of Justification obtained, but not a cause of the increase thereof; let him be anathema.

Notice that not only do good works play a part in justification according to the Roman Catholic Church, but justification itself is a matter of degree and can be increased. Here again it has defected from the teaching of Holy Scripture. It is significant that the chapter on justification in Ludwig Ott's work, to which we have already referred, is headed "The Process of Justification." However, since this confusion in Roman teaching does more damage to the doctrine of justification than of sanctification, we will say no more about it here.

Different mode of accomplishment. Whereas we are justified through faith alone, our sanctification involves both faith and effort. In the verse following our Ephesians quotation Paul goes on to speak of sanctification. Salvation is "not ... of works" but it is "for good works," and surely the very word *work* implies effort. When we are thinking of our justification, it is certainly correct to insist that "it is no good trying to be good." But when the Holy Spirit is sanctifying the sinner, it is part of the process to challenge and stimulate him or her to work and effort. As we saw in our last chapter, the work of renewal requires of the sinner not passive surrender, but active obedience. In fact, as we shall see in chapter twelve, sanctification requires considerable effort and discipline from the believer.

Table 1 brings into focus the difference between these two doctrines.

The Connection between Justification and Sanctification

Although the two doctrines must be carefully distinguished, justification and sanctification are never separated in our experience. We cannot have one without the other. Every sinner needs both, for sin never condemns a person without also defiling him. And God meets both needs, for when he saves a person he does it completely. However, many have misunderstood the inseparable nature of these two aspects of salvation, and so we turn now to emphasize that connection.

Justification	Sanctification
1. Concerns guilt	1. Concerns pollution
2. Legal, external, objective	2. Experiential, internal, subjective
3. Relates to our position	3. Relates to our condition
4. Righteousness imputed	4. Righteousness imparted
5. Has no degrees (That is, a person is either "Guilty" or "Not Guilty." No one is described as "Slightly Guilty" or "Fairly Guilty.")	5. Has degrees (That is, some have progressed in the Christian life further than others.)
6. Once-for-all and not repeated	6. A gradual process
7. By declaration of God the Father	7. By operation of the Holy Spirit
8. No place for our works	8. Our cooperation by moral exertion and personal discipline most necessary

Table 1

No sanctification without justification. To suppose that a person must become righteous before being declared righteous is a mistake of natural reasoning. Human wisdom teaches it. God has revealed that it is the other way around. In fact, until justified, a person is under God's condemnation and so is in no position to be sanctified, being yet cut off from the only one who can do it. This is how the New Testament frequently describes the position of people before they believed in Christ: "alienated . . . and strangers . . . having no hope and without God" (Eph 2:12). Before believing in Christ, no one is able to please God, for "whatever does not proceed from faith is sin" (Rom 14:23).

This is the important truth which is stressed in Article 13 of the Church of England, "Of works before justification":

Works done before the grace of Christ, and the inspiration of His Spirit, are not pleasant to God, forasmuch as they spring not of faith in Jesus Christ, neither do they make men meet to receive grace . . . yea rather, for that they are not done as God hath willed and commanded them to be done, we doubt not but they have the nature of sin.

No justification without sanctification. Some well-meaning Christians speak of being justified on one date and being sanctified some time later. Others talk about accepting Jesus as Savior and subsequently receiving him as Lord. Yet another variation on the same theme is to speak of an experience of the Holy Spirit as something quite separate and distinct from the benefits of Christ's death on the cross. Most of the forms of perfectionism we shall consider in chapter eight are based upon such a separation. Yet another misunderstanding of the doctrine of sanctification is expressed in this reasoning: "You received your justification by a simple act of faith without any effort on your part. In the same way you can be sanctified, by receiving it as a gift by simple faith."

It is important to notice that justification and sanctification are kept together in Scripture. Paul writes, "He is the source of your life in Christ Jesus, whom God made our wisdom, our righteousness [i.e., justification] and sanctification and redemption" (1 Cor 1:30). Those who are in Christ Jesus, then, have him in all these aspects. Even though there was so much moral failure in the lives of the Corinthian Christians that Paul had to describe them as carnal and not spiritual, they are still addressed as saints. That is God's very purpose in choosing us to be his people, that we should be conformed to the image of his son (Rom 8:29). "He chose us in him before the foundation of the world, that we should be holy and blameless before him" (Eph 1:4). So good works are the essential result of living faith, which is one of the main points in the letter of James (2:17-20).

The connection between the two doctrines is that sanctification is a necessary result of justification, and to imagine that a person can be justified without any moral improvement reveals a defective view of both doctrines. Warfield notes, "Sanctification is but the execution of the justifying decree. For it to fail would be for the acquitted person not to be released in accordance with his acquittal."[5] So the justifying decree of Jesus, "Neither do I condemn you," is immediately followed by the call to sanctification, "Go, and do not sin again" (Jn 8:11).

The attempt to separate justification from sanctification by a lapse of time also points to a defective view of faith in Christ. On what scriptural ground can it be asserted that we can believe for justification one day and on a later occasion believe for sanctification? Nowhere in the Bible is faith divided up like that. If justification necessarily leads to sanctification, then justifying faith is identical with sanctifying faith. That faith is faith in Christ, who is both our justification and our sanctification, rather than faith in any doctrine. We cannot fragment salvation into numerous distinct particles, each of which is to be sought and acquired by a separate act of faith.

We are not here fussing over doctrinal exactness, for the error we are considering has more sinister implications. To imagine that a person can be justified without also being sanctified is very close to the suggestion that Paul rejects so completely at the beginning of Romans 6. Indeed, the objection which Paul anticipates in the opening verse in the words, "Are we to continue in sin that grace may abound?" could well be rewritten, "Are we to neglect sanctification because of the benefits of justification?"

T. C. Hammond brings out the gravity of this implication when he writes:

Its great danger is to suggest that the work of God in justification is, if we may so express it, a bare minimum which secures salvation but does not seriously affect the life. We find such statements made as that Jesus is taken as Saviour but is not acknowledged as Lord. If this is only a loose and unguarded way of saying that many Christians live far below the great possibilities opened for them in the life of full surrender it would not be necessary to do more than point out that it is an unguarded way of speaking. But when the idea is extended to suggest that it is possible to continue in a low state of Christian living in full consciousness that there are other demands pressed upon us by God which we can afford to ignore if we merely wish to escape condemnation, and are indifferent to any crown of reward, then indeed it becomes a most serious evil and may lead people to nourish an utterly false hope."[6]

8
Perfectionism

Perfectionism is an error which is always appearing in one form or another. It states, simply, that it is possible for a Christian to live sinlessly, to be perfect in the sense of fulfilling all that God requires. This error was certainly known in the days of the early church and may well have been in Paul's mind as he wrote Philippians 3. Various forms of the teaching have also been held by the Roman Catholic Church.

All modern perfectionist movements, however, seem to stem, at least in some modified form, from the views of John Wesley, for it was Wesley who first gave the idea prominence in Protestant circles. It has been hailed by some as Wesley's distinctive contribution to the church and has even been compared with Luther's rediscovery of the doctrine of justification by faith. Wesley himself never claimed to have attained perfection. In fact, in a letter published in a London journal when he was sixty-four, he distinctly denied that he himself had ever experienced it. Many of his successors have not shown the same reticence.

Where Perfectionism Originated

Before we come to consider what the Bible teaches on this subject and to discuss the Scriptures claimed in its support, we ought to be aware of a basic presupposition underlying almost all perfectionist teaching. This is the assumption that obligation is determined by ability. Pelagius, a British monk who lived in the fourth and fifth centuries and who has given his name to the view of sin and grace known as Pelagianism, first propounded this view. His fundamental proposition was this: because God has commanded us to do what is good, we must have the ability to do it: and so we have a will which is absolutely free. In order to assert this, Pelagius had to deny any idea of a sinful nature in humanity. Sin, he taught, consists only in separate wrong acts of the will. So perfection can become a real possibility for the unaided, natural person. He can do all that God requires of him.

Some perfectionists have followed Pelagius both in his presupposition that obligation is determined by ability, and in the deductions he makes from it about the moral ability of the natural man. Charles G. Finney, for example, a perfectionist of the nineteenth century, adapted his understanding of God's law to this presupposition and even claimed to find argument for his theory in the language of the first and great commandment:

> The very language of the law is such as to level its claims to the capacity of the subject however great or small that subject may be. "Thou shalt love the Lord thy God with all thy heart, with all thy soul, with all thy mind, and with all thy strength." Here then it is plain, that all the law de-

mands, is the exercise of whatever strength we have, in the service of God. Now as entire sanctification consists in perfect obedience to the law of God, and as the law requires nothing more than the right use of whatever strength we have, it is, of course, forever settled, that a state of entire sanctification is attainable in this life, *on the ground of natural ability.*[1]

Finney's argument is, according to Gwyn Walters, based on a misunderstanding of Deuteronomy 6:5.[2] Who can be blamed for regarding Finney as a Pelagian?

However, by no means would all forms of perfectionism go so far as this. Most would apply the basic Pelagian principle only to the regenerate, to the Christian who is a partaker of God's grace. God demands from his redeemed people perfection. Such perfection must be possible to Christians or else God would not demand it from them. Some perfections draw attention to the low moral standards of many Christians (and it has of course been possible to do this in every age) and then ask, "Is this God's purpose?" If not, then some higher life must be possible. They attempt then to define what *is* possible. If it is not possible to eradicate the sinful nature, then perhaps it is possible to keep that nature under control and so live a life of constant victory. If sanctification is a matter of growth, then perhaps at every stage in our development there is a limited degree of growth that God requires—and such a degree is possible to us.

Notice that the same assumption runs through all the forms this doctrine takes: *what is demanded of us must be possible.* Yet this proposition does not occur in Scripture, which nowhere equates obligation with ability. Look, for example, at John 8. Here we find Jesus telling his hearers that they were the bondslaves of sin and unable to hear his word, and yet at the same time that they would die in their sin. Even though they were slaves to sin, God would still hold them accountable. Paul teaches precisely the same thing. Men are under obligation to God's law even though they are unable to fulfill its demands.

The absurdity of the Pelagian principle can be seen when it is applied in other directions, as B. B. Warfield demonstrates. First of all, he quotes from Finney an example of the type of argument we have been considering:

> If it is not a practicable duty to be perfectly holy in this world, then it will follow that the devil has so completely accomplished his design of corrupting mankind, that Jesus Christ is at fault, and has no way to sanctify His people but by taking them out of the world. . . . If perfect sanctification is not attainable in this world, it must be either from a want of motives in the Gospel, or a want of sufficient power in the Spirit of God.

To this Warfield replies:

> It would be a poor reader indeed who did not perceive at once that such dilemmas could be applied equally to every evil with which man is afflicted—disease, death, the uncompleted salvation of the world. If it is not a practicable thing to be perfectly well in this world, then Jesus Christ has been vanquished by the devil and has no way to make His people well except by taking them out of the world. If freedom from death is not attainable in this world, then it must be due to want of sufficient power in the Spirit of God. If the world does not become at once the pure Kingdom of God in which only righteousness dwells, then we must infer either a want of sufficient motives in the Gospel or a want of sufficient power in the Son of God. There have been people who reasoned thus: the point of interest now is, that it was not otherwise that Finney reasoned—and that accounts for many things besides his perfectionism. It is a simple matter of fact that the effects of redemption, in the individual and in the world at large, are realized, not all at once, but through a long process: and that their complete enjoyment lies only "at the end."[3]

Biblical Considerations

We now turn to the scriptural passages which are sometimes quoted in support of perfectionism. We do have, for example, commands to be perfect. Our Lord said, "You, therefore, must be perfect, as your heavenly Father is perfect" (Mt 5:48). We have already seen that our ability cannot be determined from the commandments of God. But what about cases where believers are described as perfect? We find Paul speaking of "them that are perfect" (1 Cor 2:6 KJV) and "as many as be perfect" (Phil 3:15 KJV). Notice, however, it does not say "sinlessly perfect." The word can equally be well translated "full grown" and in itself means no more than this. This is in fact how the King James Version translates it in Hebrews 5:14. The Revised Standard Version employs "mature" in all these cases except the one in Matthew.

John Wesley based his doctrine of perfection on the "perfect love" referred to in 1 John 4:17-21. But Wesley's exposition is far from clear,[4] and I find little in this passage on which to base any doctrine of sinless perfection. John R. W. Stott comments, "John is not suggesting that any Christian's love could in this life be flawlessly perfect, but rather developed and mature, set fixedly upon God."[5]

Two other verses in the same Epistle are often held out as proof texts for sinless perfection: "No one born of God commits sin" (1 Jn 3:9) and "We know that any one born of God does not sin" (1 Jn 5:18). At first sight perhaps they do appear to teach this, although if the method of interpretation is correct they really prove too much. They would mean that sinless perfection is not only possible for a Christian, but inevitable! This in itself should be enough to demonstrate that the perfectionist method of interpretation cannot be the right one.

John is here writing of something which applies to every child of God. It cannot mean that each one is sinless because he makes explicit reference to the provision God has made for believers when they do sin (see, e.g., 1 Jn 2:1-2). The most natural explanation is that John is describing here the essential nature of the new life of a Christian. Scholars have noted the present tense employed in the Greek, which expresses the idea that the one who is born of God does not go on sinning continually. This, for example, is how Berkhof understands it. "In view of the fact that John invariably uses the present to express the idea that the one born of God does not sin, it is possible that he desires to express the idea that the child of God does not go on sinning habitually, as the devil does."[6] Giving the Bible readings at the Keswick Convention in 1959 on this Epistle, E. M. Blaiklock explained it like this:

> The verse, of course, must be read in the context of the whole letter. The present tense in the Greek verb implied habit, continuity, unbroken sequence. A Christian is quite capable of sinning. That is a sad fact of common experience, and John has recognized it and named the remedy while admitting the fact. Nevertheless, opposition to sin, and hatred of it, is the ruling principle of life. A Christian may fail and fall, but the enemy has but brief triumph. The fallen rises again, confesses his fault, and presses on. The habitual sinner does none of these things. Just as the apostates who had left the Church proved, in John's view, that they had never belonged to it, so the one who "continues in sin", who covets no change, and seeks no victory, proves in the act that he had never known Christ. The true Christian echoes Paul, "Who shall deliver me from the body of this death? I thank God through Jesus Christ our Lord."[7]

It is sometimes said that John's words, "The blood of Jesus his Son cleanses us from all sin" (1 Jn 1:7), declare the possibility of an immediate and complete deliverance from the power of sin. But this interpretation fails to take into consideration the context in which the verse is found. As Stephen Neill writes on this and the previous verse, "So far from excluding the possibility of sinning, John is here presupposing it, and is indicating how this continuing reality in the life of the church is to be dealt with."[8]

The verses used to support the doctrine of sinless perfection just will not bear the weight that is placed upon them. But we can also demonstrate that the doctrine is contradicted by Scripture. For one thing, there is clear evidence that the New Testament Christians were not themselves sinlessly perfect—not even the apostles. Paul, for example, had a sharp contention with Barnabas on one occasion and with Peter on another. Moreover, we find some of the holiest men in the Bible confessing their sins. Indeed, there are clear statements that no one is sinless. Solomon declared that "there is no man who does not sin" (1 Kings 8:46), while John maintains that those who claim to the contrary are victims of self-deception (1 Jn 1:8). Sin is a constant problem to be faced in the Christian life. The spirit and the flesh contend in an unceasing conflict (Gal 5:16-24). Is it not significant that the Lord's Prayer includes prayers for forgiveness and deliverance from temptation and the evil one? Presumably these are included in the pattern prayer because they are among the normal needs of a Christian.

Variations of Perfectionism

Many who have acknowledged the untenability of absolute perfectionism, but who still cling to the Pelagian presupposition underlying it, have suggested some modifications to this doctrine. The alternative theories, all based on the assumption that obligation is determined by opportunity, are distinguished by their various assessments of the moral capability of a Christian. Their exponents search the Scriptures to see if a formula exists whereby their own particular type of perfectionism may be obtained. They often strongly contest sinless perfection, recognizing it to be well beyond human reach in this life, without realizing that their alternative propositions really amount to the same thing in another form.

Some common features. There are a number of theories, perhaps almost as many theories as there are exponents, but one or two features are common to them all. They all understand sanctification to be an isolated experience that occurs after justification. Just as justification is received from God by an act of faith, so is sanctification received by another separate and specific act of faith. This interpretation is hardly in keeping with the biblical usage of these terms, as we have already observed.

Second, these theories tend to externalize sin. They fail to do justice to the inward corruption of human nature which we considered in chapter four. According to one view, present sanctification consists in keeping the sinful nature under control and in subjection. *Counteraction* is the word often used to describe this. Some preachers have boldly offered believers the possibility of living "a life of constant victory" with the inner sinful nature kept under control. It is difficult to distinguish this view from perfectionism except that the latter is limited to eradicating external acts of sin.

Of course, there is a truth contained in it. Present sanctification most certainly does include keeping our sinful nature in subjection. After all, does not Paul enjoin his readers to "make no provision for the flesh, to gratify its desires" (Rom 13:14)? However, this is only part of the truth, and this part alone would give a poor conception of salvation in Christ. This view overlooks the inward character of sin which we faced in chapter four, and the fact that sanctification is as much concerned with the sinful nature as with external acts. Renewal, as we saw in chapter six, is an inward work, and Paul speaks of God sanctifying us wholly, which includes our whole spirit, soul and body (1 Thess 5:23). Sanctification is a radical transformation brought about in man's innermost being and nature. The Holy Spirit "makes the tree good that the fruit may be good."[9]

Another frequent tendency of these theories is to lower the standard of holiness. It may be the only way to substantiate a claim to perfection! Proponents suggest that God requires less of us under grace than he did under law. Obviously this unscriptural notion could be a very dangerous one. Indeed, history shows many examples of perfectionism leading to low moral standards among Christians and even scandalous behavior. Handley Moule observed this phenomenon:

Such views are not uncommonly attended, in those who hold them, by a certain oblivion to personal shortcomings and inconsistencies; by an obscuration of consciousness, and of conscience, more or less marked, towards the sinfulness of ordinary, everyday violations of the law of holiness in respect of "meekness, humbleness of mind, long-suffering", sympathy, and other quiet graces.[10]

Perhaps this is not really surprising. A doctrinaire clinging to perfection, despite practical evidence to the contrary, can lead a person to assume that all he does must be right, and so, to use the forceful phrase of J. S. Whale, "Belief in the inner light may be the shortest road to the outer darkness." Or, as Stephen Neill wrote, "It might almost seem as though, under the judgment of God, the highest claims prepared the way for the deepest falls."[11]

One particularly ingenious idea is that perfection involves freedom from conscious sinning. Again we refer back to our chapter on sin to refute this, and again point out how important it is to have a right understanding of sin in order to have a correct view of holiness. I describe this view as "ingenious" because it provides a way of combining some form of perfection with that of Christian growth. The idea is that in this life we come short of the holiness of Christ. But we can be perfect to the best of our limited knowledge. Growth in grace means the progressive uncovering of our unconscious sinfulness, and as this proceeds, so the blood of Christ cleanses us.

As Pearsall Smith, a nineteenth-century advocate of the view, explained, " 'The blood cleanseth'—is ever cleansing sin *from the conscience*, as it is progressively revealed." B. B. Warfield, to whom we are indebted for this quotation, adds, "which is not exactly what 1 John i. 7 says."[12] Our conscience's dictates do not form the biblical standard by which our perfection is to be judged. B. B. Warfield has surely put his finger right on the weakness of the whole theory when he writes:

> The standard being a subjective, not an objective one, our knowledge, not God's law, Christian perfection does not mean the fulfilling of all that God requires of a Christian, but only of all that a Christian's conscience, in its changing degrees of knowledge, requires from time to time of himself. The subjectiveness of the thought is intense, and one is tempted to apply the proverb, "Where ignorance is bliss, 'tis folly to be wise."[13]

Stages of perfection?　　Closely connected with this view and often combined with it is yet another modification of perfectionism. It supposes that Christians can be perfect at every stage of their development. What they are growing toward is not perfection, because they have this already, but rather maturity. This view became popular at the end of the last century largely through a book which enjoyed an enormous circulation on both sides of the Atlantic. It compared the Christian to a growing baby or a maturing apple, as the following extract shows:

> The little babe may be all that a babe could be, or ought to be, and may therefore perfectly please its mother; and yet it is very far from being what that mother would wish it to be when the years of maturity shall come.
>
> The apple in June is a perfect apple for June; it is the best apple that June can produce: but it is very different from the apple in October, which is a perfected apple.[14]

Again the view of sin and of the corruption of human nature

is completely inadequate. B. B. Warfield spots the basic error and shows the unsuitability of the analogy. "The human 'apple in June' is not merely an immature apple, it is a rotten apple. It does not merely need 'to grow' in order to become the 'perfected' apple of October, it has got to be remade before it becomes the perfect apple for June and is in a state to 'grow' at all."[15]

The first analogy is no more appropriate. A growing child *may* "perfectly please its mother," but that depends not only on the child but also on the standards and perception of the mother. Because fallen, no child or baby is at any stage all it "could be or ought to be." To regard the Christian life as a process of growth is quite scriptural, but to view every stage of growth as perfection is quite inappropriate for a Christian whose nature is corrupt and worldly and is always in conflict with God's Spirit.

The question is, By what standard are our lives to be judged? Stephen Neill is right to ask, "Is man once again to be the measure of all things? By what standard am I to be judged? Is my unaided capacity at any one moment to be the measure at that moment of Christian attainment and Christian expectation?"[16]

Biblical Perfectionism

In facing the errors of a false perfectionism, we must not lose sight of what the Bible does teach on this subject. We have seen that the word *perfect* means "mature." Are we really seeking the maturity of which the Bible speaks? Are we showing the maturity of those who are skillful in the Word of God (Heb 5:11-14)? Are we showing the stability which accompanies maturity, or are we still the children Paul describes as "tossed to and fro and carried about with every wind of doctrine" (Eph 4:14)? While perfectionism may be an error of doctrine, its exponents have often given a much needed emphasis. Perfectionist movements often arise as a protest against the low Christian morality and commitment. Sinless perfection may not be attainable in this life, but it is nonetheless the goal. It is not difficult to see the dangers possible in the attitude which says, "Well, of course, we cannot be perfect, can we?"

"One cannot fob off Perfectionism by saying 'In many things we all stumble' (James 3:2) or 'Wretched man that I am! who shall deliver me...?' (Romans 7:24), for these utterances are not excuses for sin but confessions of sin."[17] Far worse than the assumption of sinless perfection is complacency over sinful imperfection. The right balance is carefully maintained in Scripture. Take the first Epistle of John, for example; one moment the writer is warning us that "if we say we have no sin, we deceive ourselves, and the truth is not in us." A moment later he is urging, "I am writing this to you so that you may not sin" (1:8; 2:1). Here is the attitude of heart that is to be ours. The aim of a Christian should always be *not* to sin. Paul knew something of this, too. Having set aside all claims to perfection, he declared that nonetheless perfection was his goal. "One thing I do," he wrote, "Forgetting those things which are behind, and reaching forth unto those things which are before, I press toward the mark for the prize of the high calling of God in Christ Jesus." The following verse puts Paul's statement right into the context of our subject: "Let us therefore, as many as be perfect, be thus minded" (Phil 3:13-15 KJV).

High aims and ideals are always important to a Christian. Stephen Neill detects a similarity between the Christian and the artist at this point:

We can learn a religious truth from the artists. The great among them have ever striven for a perfection of expression that they knew could never be attained—and in the ever-frustrated effort have left us monuments of their greatness. Others have early attained a certain slick perfection of technique; and have made it astonishingly plain to us how banal even excellent painting can be, if uninspired by the ideal that ever flees before the questing eye and hand of the artist.[18]

John, in 1 John 2:1, not only holds before us the ideal of sinlessness; he also gives advice toward the attainment of that ideal. This, he says, is one of the purposes in his writing. "I am writing *this* to you so that you may not sin." We naturally ask, "What is *this?*" and of course in answering the question we could well study the whole Bible, to which the word *this* clearly applies. What, however, is John pointing to in the immediate context of his Epistle? It is surely to three important facts, which he mentioned in the previous chapter. The facts are presented here in the form of three mistakes a Christian is to avoid.

First of all, a Christian should avoid having a wrong view of God (1 Jn 1:5-6). The error exposed in verse 6 amounts to this, that sin does not really matter. It is based on an idea that God is very easygoing. "God is light and in him is no darkness at all" is replaced by "God is nice and in him is no nastiness at all"! This, however, comes a long way short of the Bible view of God's holiness. God cannot tolerate sin in any form; he cannot possibly coexist with our sin. So in verse 6 John is underlining the truth that anybody who wants to take an easygoing view of God and a careless attitude toward sin will find that fellowship with God is impossible. Fellowship with God means sharing God's antagonism to sin. A right attitude toward God lies at the very heart of Christian living and is essential to spiritual health. It imparts a sense of responsibility to our living.

Second, we must not underestimate the importance of the principle of sin working within us. In addition to the inadequate views of our sinful nature we considered already, there are the popular psychological theories held in the world. Sin ceases to be sin. Instead of a sinner being a wrongdoer who deserves to be punished, he is regarded as suffering from a disease and deserving of pity. Now, of course, where responsibility begins and ends in some cases can be a great problem. But we do need to guard the full biblical doctrine as far as our own lives are concerned.

Third, we have to avoid the pitfall of saying that "we have no sin." Such a view is serious because, as John points out, it contradicts the very Word of God. It can be expressed in many ways. One is simply through carelessness, just not bothering about the sins that mar and spoil our lives. In many Christians there is a built-in refusal to admit the possibility of being wrong and a desire, if it is possible, to dodge the accusing finger. We can always find excuses to shelter behind to remove all sense of guilt. Christians who want to make progress toward the goal before them must pay continual attention to the details of their lives, including not only what they do but the words they say, the way they say them and the way they even think. They have to be on the lookout for the little foxes "that spoil the vineyards" (Song 2:15). They must be willing to face individual and specific sins.

Above all we must keep in sight the perfection we already possess—the perfection which is ours in Christ. There is nothing incomplete about what he has done for us. Christ declared of his sacrifice on the cross, "It is finished." "By a single offering he has perfected for all time those who are sanctified" (Heb 10:14). It is the practical results of this perfection that we are called upon to work out in our lives until the day when we are "unblamable in holiness ... at the coming of our Lord Jesus with his saints" (1 Thess 3:13).

9
Christian
Growth

If *we cannot reach perfection* and complete sanctification during this life, then what *can* we hope for? Scripture teaches that the Christian life is one of growth. Here is the vital positive truth to put in the place of the error I have tried to expose. Growth is what the apostle Paul so often looks for in the lives of his readers. He urges it, prays for it and, where there is evidence of it, he thanks God.

Rather, speaking the truth in love, we are to grow up in every way into him. (Eph 4:15)

And it is my prayer that your love may abound more and more. (Phil 1:9)

We are bound to give thanks to God always for you . . . because your faith is growing abundantly. (2 Thess 1:3)

Its Emphasis in Scripture

Other New Testament writers express the same desire for their readers. The second Epistle of Peter closes with a call to "grow in the grace and knowledge of our Lord and Savior Jesus Christ" (2 Pet 3:18). The writer to the Hebrews urges, "Let us . . . go on to maturity" (Heb 6:1).

The writers of the New Testament assume that Christians will make progress in their experience of God and in the holiness of their lives. They do not suggest that what Christians need is one decisive act of consecration at some time subsequent to their conversion. Unfortunately, many have thought that one such decision would do it, and they have been sadly disillusioned. But as T. C. Hammond has pointed out, "The whole tenor of Scripture is against the idea that one supreme act of decision secures to us permanently all the blessing of sanctification."[1] Growth is one of the marks of health in a man's spiritual life, as it is in the physical lives of animals and plants. Indeed, lack of growth, or immaturity, often causes defects in the Christian's life. Inability to use Holy Scripture is one example of this, and the writer to the Hebrews compares the person who lacks progress in this to an unweaned baby (Heb 5:11-13). Instability is viewed in the same way, and Paul calls upon us "that we may no longer be children, tossed to and fro and carried about with every wind of doctrine, by the cunning of men, by their craftiness in deceitful wiles. Rather, speaking the truth in love, we are to grow up in every way into him who is the head, into Christ" (Eph 4:14-15). The carnal Christians in Corinth are called "babes in Christ." Their spiritual immaturity lies at the bottom of the divisions for which Paul criticizes them (1 Cor 3:1-9).

Recognizing the place of growth in the Christian life should lead to one or two practical effects. It should challenge the complacent. If the Christian life is from beginning to end intended to be one of steady growth, those who imagine that they have arrived at some superior state of holiness need to be shaken out of their superiority. This side of heaven there will always be more ground to be possessed, and people who imagine otherwise may be in a rut and may have been there for years. On the other hand, for the disheartened, this teaching on growth may come as a great comfort. Those who are deeply conscious of where they fall short, and who are discouraged at their apparent lack of spiritual attainment, need to be reminded that in the Christian life everything does not come at once. Because sanctification is a process, better things lie ahead if they will persevere in the proper use of the means of growth which we shall discuss later in this chapter.

Ways in Which We Grow

We will now be more specific about how we grow. First of all, however, there are two ways in which we do not grow. As has been pointed out in chapter seven, there is no growth in our justification before God. Whether Christians have only just been converted or have believed in Jesus Christ for forty years makes no difference as far as their justification is concerned. This is not a matter of degree. We are either justified or not justified. We are either objects of God's favor or objects of his wrath and condemnation. We are like the prisoner in the dock who is either declared "Guilty" or "Not Guilty," but never "Fairly Guilty." The same can be said of regeneration, the first stage in sanctification. As we saw in chapter six, people either possess spiritual life or they do not, and once those who have been dead in sin have been quickened by the Holy Spirit of God, they will never be any more regenerate than they are then. After all, a thirty-year-old person is no more alive than a newborn baby.

On the other hand, the Bible shows that in certain distinctive aspects of the Christian life growth is to be expected. Most references to Christian growth have to do with the increase of our faith and love, but there are others too.

Growth in grace (2 Pet 3:18).   A Christian lives in the realm of grace. All he is and hopes for is not according to his own merit or deserving, but is due to the free, unmerited favor of God. So a growing Christian is one who experiences more and more of God's grace and favor.

This is what Peter means when he expresses the wish that grace should be multiplied to his readers (1 Pet 1:2 and 2 Pet 1:2). Not that the grace of God itself is capable of increase, but, as Alan Stibbs remarks, "that his readers may increase in personal experience of the character and benefit of God's dealings with men in Christ and by the Spirit."[2] So Christians who are growing in their experience of the grace of God will have a correspondingly deepening awareness of the sinfulness of their own nature and their need of God's mercy. The apostle Paul shows his own growth in grace in regarding himself as "the very least of all the saints" (Eph 3:8), and the foremost of sinners (1 Tim 1:15). As Christians grow in sanctification, they become more conscious of the need for God's forgiveness. The virtue of humility is inseparable from true godliness. Bishop Ryle observes of the growing Christian:

> The riper he is for glory, the more, like the ripe corn, he hangs down his head. The brighter and clearer is his light, the more he sees of the shortcomings and infirmities of his own heart. When first converted, he would tell you he saw but little of them compared to what he sees now. Would anyone know whether he is growing in grace? Be sure that you look within for increased humility.[3]

Growth in knowledge (2 Pet 3:18).   The Christian grows in the knowledge of spiritual things, not necessarily in worldly wisdom. Knowledge of the latter kind merely "puffs up," as Paul had to remind the Corinthians (1 Cor 8:1). Spurgeon once aptly observed that swelling is not growing. However, a knowledge of spiritual things and supremely of God himself is an indispensable part of the deepening of our Christian experience. Paul gives as his great aim in life, "that I may know him" (Phil 3:10). Such knowledge is the characteristic mark of maturity that the apostle John attributes to "fathers" (1 Jn 2:13-14).

Growth in faith. Scripture has much to say about growth in faith (see, e.g., Lk 17:5-6; 2 Cor 10:15; 2 Thess 1:3). The strength of our faith has a great deal to do with the extent of our sanctification. Here, incidentally, is a further difference between justification and sanctification. For justification a weak faith is quite sufficient, as John Berridge, an evangelical leader in the eighteenth century, observed in a letter. "Remember also that salvation does not depend on the *strength* of faith, but the *reality* of it. In the gospels, Jesus often rebukes weak faith, but never rejects it. Weak faith brings but little comfort, yet is as much entitled to salvation as strong."[4]

The man in the Gospels with the demon-possessed boy discovered the truth of this. Basically, he believed in Jesus, but his was a weak faith, easily hindered by the atmosphere of unbelief in which he lived and by the failure of Christ's disciples. Yet he found when he approached Jesus with the words "I believe; help my unbelief," that Jesus granted him his request (Mk 9:24). And so it is for justification. The person whose faith is still at the stage expressed by the hymn "I hold Thee with a trembling hand" can be certain that this is faith enough to bring peace with God.

But for progress in the Christian life it is a very different story, for then the strength of a person's faith most certainly does matter. In the precise, theological language of Berkhof, "While even the weakest faith mediates a perfect justification, the degree of sanctification is commensurate with the strength of the Christian's faith and the persistence with which he apprehends Christ."[5] There are many examples of such faith in Scripture, such as the long list of Old Testament saints in Hebrews 11. Why was it that these Old Testament men lived such effective lives for God? Because they were men of faith—as we are repeatedly told throughout the chapter. They did not just have the bare minimum of faith whereby they could receive the grace of God, but they were, as we are told in the case of Abraham, *strong* in faith. How different this is from the theory that justification and sanctification are received by different and separate acts of faith! As the faith we already possess deepens and grows stronger in response to God's grace, we progress in the life God has given us to live.

Growth in love.   Love is the gift that we are to seek above all others, and without it all our Christian activity and good works are useless in God's sight (1 Cor 13). Being filled with love is the most distinctive mark of Christian maturity (1 Cor 13:11), so it is hardly surprising that so many of the references to growth have to do with love (see, e.g., Phil 1:9; 1 Thess 3:12; 4:9-12). Notice, by the way, that this love is not to be an undiscerning charity but should be combined with "knowledge and all discernment" (Phil 1:9).

Growth in character and life.   As we increase in knowledge, faith and love, so we develop in Christian character and Christlikeness. It is the result of all the other aspects of growth. Our Christian living and service become increasingly effective and pleasing to God. Paul urges the Thessalonians, "Finally, brethren, we beseech and exhort you . . . as you learned from us how you ought to live and to please God, just as you are doing, you do so more and more" (1 Thess 4:1). We become increasingly like Christ, for we grow "to the measure of the stature of the fullness of Christ" and "grow up in every way into him who is the head, into Christ" (Eph 4:13, 15). As we daily occupy ourselves with the things of Christ, so we are gradually changed "into his likeness from one degree of glory to another: for this comes from the Lord who is the Spirit" (2 Cor 3:18).

The Nature of Growth
Why is the Christian life one of progressive growth? Is it

that God's blessing is held back and only portioned out to us in degrees? Not at all. In Ephesians 1 we read that God has "blessed us in Christ with every spiritual blessing in the heavenly places" (v. 3). This is an accomplished fact. If we have Christ then we have everything God has for us, and he has held nothing back.

What we need is not for God to give us anything "held back," but rather to be made aware of all that is ours in Christ and then fully to appropriate it. It is for this that Paul prays in Ephesians. In the first prayer in chapter 1 he seeks a greater awareness of all that God has done, together with the enlightenment which this demands (vv. 15-23). Then in the second prayer (3:16-21) he goes on to pray for a full experience of all this through the indwelling of Jesus Christ by his Spirit. On this basis the Christian life is to be lived.

Having shown in the first three chapters the greatness of our calling in Christ and the wonder of it all, Paul introduces the practical section at the beginning of chapter 4 with the words, "I... beg you to lead a life worthy of the calling to which you have been called." One can readily detect echoes of the Ephesian Epistle in the words of Herbert W. Cragg:

> Our contention then is well-founded when we stress the importance of a comprehensive view of our salvation. There can be no subdividing of Christ, and whatever subdivisions are needed in our consideration of Him must be due to the slowness of our hearts to grasp, or our minds to comprehend, all the fullness that we have in Him.[6]

We have found here an answer to our question. The Christian needs to grow because of the imperfect way in which he or she has understood and responded to the gospel and all its implications. This is clear in the various aspects of a Christian's growth we have already discovered from Scripture. Most of them are in some way a growth in response to God and his truth. For example, we grow in knowledge as we devote ourselves to the truth which God has revealed. Faith is our response to God's grace, while our love is our response to his love, for "we love, because he first loved us" (1 Jn 4:19).

Paul writes about his deficient response to Jesus Christ in Philippians 3:12: "Not that I have already obtained this or am already perfect; but I press on to make it my own, because Christ Jesus has made me his own." Notice that Paul here confesses that despite all that God has thus far done in his life, and even though Christ has taken the initiative and fully laid hold of him (i.e., "Christ Jesus has made me his own"), he himself has not fully obtained or laid hold of everything that Christ has for him. J. B. Phillips makes Paul's meaning especially clear. He paraphrases it as:

> Yet, my brothers, I do not consider myself to have "arrived," spiritually, nor do I consider myself already perfect. But I keep going on, grasping ever more firmly that purpose for which Christ Jesus grasped me. My brothers, I do not consider myself to have fully grasped it even now. But I do concentrate on this: I leave the past behind and with hands outstretched to whatever lies ahead I go straight for the goal—my reward the honor of my high calling by God in Christ Jesus. (vv. 12-14)

Mercifully, by God's grace we can be justified through an imperfect faith (and who of us would dare to claim that our faith is perfect?), but we must never rest content with this. We should be like Paul who said, "I press on to make it my own, because Christ Jesus has made me his own." Early in the chapter he has gloried in his spiritual *position*. "But when he comes to speak of his spiritual *condition* the possessing thought is that all is imperfect and progressive. He has a perfect blessing; but he is an imperfect recipient of it; he has 'not attained.' "[7]

Now all this has a most important bearing on the kind of claims Christians are entitled to make concerning their spiritual attainments. In view of the considerations above it is surely inappropriate for any Christian to suggest that he or she has made a *perfect* or *complete* response to the grace of God. Claims to have *fully* surrendered or yielded one's life to God have no counterparts in the pages of holy Scripture; in view of what Paul says in the passage we have just studied, it is hard to imagine that he would have ever made them. Aware of his deficiencies, Paul has no satisfaction in the stage of progress he has reached.

Paul's attitude toward Christian growth is worth our noting. He is not discouraged by his incomplete sanctification. Rather he pushes on with single-mindedness toward a sure goal. He sets about to take a firmer hold of all that Christ has for him. To begin with, he describes in Philippians 3 his quest as *"one* thing I do," not *many* things—the very opposite of the diffusion against which the apostle James warns us: "A double-minded man [is] unstable in all his ways" (Jas 1:8). Paul is not going to fall into that trap, and so his whole life is unified around the one purpose of pressing toward the goal of the upward call of God.

Paul also tells us that he is forward looking, "forgetting what lies behind and straining forward to what lies ahead" (Phil 3:13). There are some great blessings in the former part of his life, but he does not allow these to make him complacent; he does not rest content with what he already has. He is like the athlete whose eye is fixed on the winning tape. When he says "I press on toward the goal," the verb is one used of the hunter and also of the athlete who strains every nerve to achieve his object. This is the attitude of the growing Christian.

The word most often used for the growth of a Christian in the New Testament is *auxanō*, which is the word normally used of organic growth. In other words, a Christian grows from within as a living organism. John Owen observes the way in which Scripture so frequently compares the Christian's growth in grace and holiness to the growth of trees and plants.

> These trees and plants have the principle of their growth in themselves. They do not grow immediately from external adventitious aid, but from their own seminal virtue and radical moisture. It is no otherwise in the progress of holiness; it has a root, a seed, a principle of growth in the soul. All grace is immortal seed, and contains in it a living growing principle, John 4:14. That which has not in itself a life and power of growth, is not grace. And therefore whatever duties men perform, as directed by natural light, or urged by convictions from the word, if they proceed not from a principle of spiritual life in the heart, they are not fruits of holiness.[8]

It is important to notice the depth at which a Christian grows. It is not just a matter of forming fresh habits in life, although this may well have to take place. Rather, Christian growth is internal and springs from the innermost being of the Christian where the Holy Spirit of God is at work. Growth which is nothing more than the forming of fresh habits could be like tying fruit to the branches of a tree—utterly superficial.

This leads on naturally to another comparison which John Owen makes:

> The growth of trees and plants is secret and imperceptible, and discerned only in the effects and consequences of it; the most watchful eye can discern little of its motion; and so it is in the progress of holiness. It is not immediately discernible either by those in whom it is, or by others who observe it, except by its fruits and effects.[9]

Now let us apply all this to the way in which a Christian's faith grows. It is shown very strikingly in Luke 17:5-6. The apostles, having recognized the importance of their faith, ask the Lord, "Increase our faith!" The Greek word for "increase" is significant. It is not *auxanō* but *prostithēmi*. This may imply that they were asking our Lord to add to their faith in the way bricks are added to a building by someone, externally. It may just mean "Grant us faith." Whichever is the case, there is no uncertainty about Jesus' reply. He spoke of faith in organic terms, comparing true faith to a grain of mustard seed. "If you had faith as a grain of mustard seed, you could say to this sycamine tree, 'Be rooted up, and be planted in the sea,' and it would obey you." True faith may be very small like a grain of mustard seed, but it possesses life with all its possibilities.

Campbell Morgan illustrates this by the story of a remarkable tomb he saw in Italy. Its occupant had left instructions in his will that a large mass of granite should be laid over it, so that if there were ever a resurrection, it would not affect him! As it happened, an acorn was dropped by a bird just before the block was lowered. Eventually the acorn germinated and grew. Such was the power of the life within it that the stone was split in two and an oak tree grew up through the crack, gradually separating the two halves of granite. If our faith is like that, if it is more than a dead orthodoxy, if it is living, then it possesses enormous potentialities and can move mountains, however small it may appear to be.

Means of Growth
If Christian growth is organic, then it needs the right food and the right conditions. Campbell Morgan's acorn germinated because it had warmth and moisture underneath the slab of granite. What does Christian growth require?

The Word of God.   Surely the supreme need is for the food of God's Word. "Long for the pure spiritual milk," writes Peter, "that by it you may grow" (1 Pet 2:2).

Not knowing God's truth is one of the most common causes of immaturity and instability. Notice how these two conditions are brought together when Peter speaks of those who are "ignorant and unstable" (2 Pet 3:16). Says Thomas Watson, a seventeenth-century English minister, "Such as are unlearned in the main points of divinity are unstable. As the body cannot be strong that has the sinews shrunk; so neither can that Christian be strong in religion who wants the grounds of knowledge, which are the sinews to strengthen and stablish him."[10]

The immature and unstable Christian does not necessarily need to make some specific act of consecration, although some may do so, but may well be simply in need of teaching. It means, too, that when Christians read their Bible, they ought to take a long-term view. They are not merely looking for a thought to help them through the next twenty-four hours, although if it so happens that what is read has particular application to circumstances at the time, this is all to the good. But primarily they are deepening their understanding of God and his ways with people as revealed in the Bible and, in consequence, seeing to it that their whole lives and outlook are molded by it. At the same time, of course, Christians must see to it that they make immediate response to everything they learn from the Bible. As James shows, we are to be "doers of the word, and not hearers only" (Jas 1:22-25). God's Word does not promote spiritual growth if its study is only intellectual. It is to be obeyed because scriptural holiness is practical and covers "all your conduct" (1 Pet 1:15).

The troubles of life. Paul warned the converts of his first missionary journey that we often "through many tribulations... must enter the kingdom of God" (Acts 14:22). Trials and difficulties are regarded as means of growth toward maturity. Scripture assumes that the Christian life is lived in a world not conducive to spiritual life. Christians can expect persecution and tribulation, and in this they are simply following in the steps of the Master. God uses these experiences to develop Christian character. Indeed, without them a Christian may become like a greenhouse plant that has never been toughened. Look, for example, at Romans 5:3-5 where, because the trials of life can profit a Christian, Paul is able to claim, "We rejoice in our sufferings." We see the same effect in James 1:2-4.

Our faith can benefit from our trials, as the example from James shows. It is like a precious metal which needs to be refined and purified from dross. Sometimes our faith is marred by biases and prejudices. Often it is vague, softened by shallow sentimentality. Yet, as we have seen in this chapter, a growing faith is vital to our sanctification. How, then, is it to be refined? Often it is by persecution or another form of tribulation. And faith, if it is real, like a metal will come to no harm. Only the dross will be burned away, "that the genuineness of your faith, more precious than gold which though perishable is tested by fire, may redound to praise and glory and honour at the revelation of Jesus Christ" (1 Pet 1:7).

The fellowship of the church.   A third means of growth for each Christian is the community of the whole body of believers, especially in the local church. The "building up of the body of Christ" will last "until we all attain... to mature manhood, to the measure of the stature of the fullness of Christ" (Eph 4:12-13). One reason why Timothy, young as he was, won the confidence of Paul to be entrusted with important missions was that he could work with others (see Phil 2:19-23). A Christian life lived in isolation from other Christians is defective, and being unable to work with others is a sign of immaturity. While some outstanding Christian leaders may have been individualists, I would suggest that this limitation nevertheless impaired their usefulness in the kingdom.

The fellowship of other Christians is an aid which no growing believer can afford to be without. It is God's will that we grow in holiness not as isolated individuals but as members of the body of Christ. It is the church, not isolated individuals, that Peter describes as "a holy priesthood" and "a holy nation" (1 Pet 2:5, 9), and which Paul sees as the household of God growing into a holy temple in the Lord (Eph 2:19-22). We need to keep in mind that our study of holiness draws heavily from the New Testament Epistles, and these were addressed not to individuals but to churches. We need fellowship as a burning coal needs the touch of other coals. Remove it from the fire and it will gradually turn dull and cold, but left with the other coals in the fire it will continue to glow with them. We need to meet regularly with our fellow Christians for worship, fellowship and instruction, that we "stir up one another to love and good works, not neglecting to meet together, as is the habit of some, but encouraging one another" (Heb 10:24-25). "Stir up" is a strong phrase and normally used in a bad sense (e.g., the dissension between Paul and Barnabas in Acts 15:39) and translated "provoke," as in the King James Version. Here it has a more pleasant sense and conveys the idea of bringing the best out of each other. We do this by the example of our lives, by sharing with one another what God has done for us and by caring for each other. All of us from time to time suffer setbacks in our Christian growth. The fellowship of the church is meant to come to our aid. "Brethren," writes the apostle, "if a man is overtaken in any trespass you who are spiritual should restore him in a spirit of gentleness" (Gal 6:1).

Among us should be "pastors and teachers" (Eph 4:11). Paul clearly sees this provision as vital to the health of the church, because as they "equip the saints for the work of the ministry" so the maturity of the church results (vv. 12-16). "Pastors" and "teachers" share the same article in the Greek, so presumably it is expected that these two ministries will be exercised by the same people. We are repeatedly told in the New Testament that the pastor's task is to feed the flock, and he will do this by his teaching. When this provision is not available in the local church the whole body will be undernourished.

At this juncture a word of caution may be necessary. Much

as we need teachers in God's Word, we should not allow ourselves to be dominated by the personalities of others, or to become overdependent on them. Personality domination is one of the prominent features of many cults in which members are required to submit to an authority structure that demands complete and unquestioning obedience in beliefs and practice. The pressures of modern life give rise to increasing emotional problems among people, and some consequently need to depend on others. They may well transfer their dependency to those whom they respect in the church. They will rely upon them to tell them exactly what to believe and how to make decisions. Yet if a Christian is to develop toward maturity, such dependency must be outgrown. The church is a caring community, but it is not a mark of grace for a Christian constantly to want care. A mature Christian is more ready to give care than to receive it, and to love without waiting to be loved. Every Christian has a ministry to exercise within the body of Christ and for this the work of the pastors and teachers is needed, "to equip the saints for the work of the ministry, for building up the body of Christ" (Eph 4:12).

The problem of dominant personalities appeared in the troubled church at Corinth. Paul was clearly disturbed by the hero worship which was being directed at church leaders, himself included, and by the party spirit which surrounded it. It was a sign of immaturity and carnality (1 Cor 3:1-4). The church undoubtedly needs an authority structure if its affairs are to be properly ordered, and the New Testament makes full provision for this. But that does not mean that those in authority should dominate the immature or encourage them to become personally dependent on them. Surely Paul meant just this when he made the disclaimer to the Corinthian church, "Not that we lord it over your faith" (2 Cor 1:24). He shows the same concern over the church at Philippi (Phil 2:12-13). It is not that they should become independent of his teaching, any more than we should. If that were so he would hardly have written them a letter so full of instruction. What concerns him is the effect that his presence has on them. He wants their Christian obedience to be no less when he is away from them than when he is there to keep his eye on them. They are to work out a salvation that is truly their own, relying on God himself working in their hearts.

10
Stimulants
to
Growth

The Christian life normally progresses by steady growth, and Scripture encourages us to expect it to be so. What then do we make of the Christian who claims to have experienced a sudden and decisive change subsequent to conversion, perhaps at a convention or because of some personal crisis, which has given him or her greater victory over sin than ever before?

The "Second Blessing"
An experience of this kind can be compatible with the steady growth normative of the Christian life. A Christian will sometimes make more progress than at other times as the result of attending a meeting or reading a particularly helpful

book. John Owen calls these the "sudden gusts and motions" and the "intense vigorous actings of grace on great occasions."[1] They are like the opening of buds and flowers. What can be misleading, however, is referring to such an experience as "*the* Second Blessing." Some people assume that such an experience is a normal part of every Christian's life and think that any Christian who has not had it ought to seek it because it is essential to living the Christian life as God intended it to be lived. As a result, many Christians have been put through unnecessary anxiety, trying to experience something they were probably never intended to have.

Christian experience is not necessarily the same thing as the experience of some Christians! I do not mean by this that any sudden turning point in a Christian's life is to be considered spurious. Trying to explain away parts of other Christians' testimonies is rarely a profitable pursuit, and unbelievers are masters of it. What I am saying is this: such experiences may be perfectly valid for the person who has them, but they are never meant to be regarded as the norm for all Christians. Still less should other Christians be urged to seek such crises for themselves. Surely the ground for what we believe about the Christian life is the Bible, not another person's experience. The only kind of experience we have any right to press on others is what Scripture clearly teaches.

Some booklets and tracts have fallen into this error. In them the authors fill most of the space writing about themselves and their experiences. They tell how their lives had been defeated, lacking in blessing, and how they went through some experience which effected a change in their lives, leading them to greater victory. They then interpret Scripture in the light of their experience and urge it on all Christians.

Samuel Chadwick, a popular writer earlier this century, used this approach of putting experience before Scripture. His chapter "Do the Scriptures teach a Second Blessing?"

makes the unpromising start, "It is easier to prove the doctrine of a Second Blessing from John Wesley than from the Bible." He gets over this difficulty through some curious reasoning. "The Second Blessing is not in a text; it is in the whole Bible. Because the man who has found it sees it everywhere, it is difficult for him to prove it anywhere." We can see this blessing, for example, "in Exodus and Leviticus; in the architecture, furniture, and ordinances of the tabernacle; as well as in distinctions of speech that seem forced and fanciful."[2] Isn't it extraordinary that Scripture is not clearer on what has been claimed to be necessary for every Christian? One would have thought that the New Testament letters, written to many who would have benefited from such an experience, might have been more explicit.

Many people fail to understand their own experience. They speak of being blessed, but are unable to be any more specific. Sometimes an upsurge of emotion in a meeting is regarded as evidence of blessing. Some people, having stayed for an after-meeting, experience great relief when their embarrassment is overcome and feel, in consequence, that they have been blessed. The only safe thing to do is to interpret all these experiences in the light of Scripture and not vice versa.

Judged by Scripture, some examples of "second blessing" could be more accurately described as conversion. This is especially true for those whose original professions of faith came in response to an appeal to "come to Jesus" with no mention of repentance. J. C. Ryle made this same observation in the introduction to his book on holiness.

Are they not, when they urge on believers the "higher life" as a second conversion, underrating the length, and breadth, and depth, and height, of that great first change which Scripture calls the new birth, the new creation, the spiritual resurrection? I may be mistaken. But I have sometimes thought, while reading the strong language used by many about "consecration", in the last few years, that those who use it must have had previously a singularly low and inadequate view of "conversion," if indeed they knew anything about conversion at all. In short, I have almost suspected that when they were *consecrated*, they were in reality *converted* for the first time![3]

Accepting Jesus as Lord. Conversion has been belittled by Christians who separate "accepting Jesus as Savior" from "accepting Jesus as Lord." They suggest that the latter comes some time subsequent to conversion. But is this really scriptural? Do we ever find New Testament writers urging their Christian readers to accept Christ as Lord? The answer is no; the writers assume that it has already taken place—at conversion. This, for example, is how Paul spoke of the Christian life. "As therefore you received Christ Jesus the Lord, so live in him, rooted and built up in him and established in the faith, just as you were taught, abounding in thanksgiving" (Col 2:6-7). The early Christians would have been quite surprised to hear "Jesus as Lord" was a second experience. For them it was a baptismal confession! So Paul does not appeal to the Colossians, "As therefore you have had a second experience, so live in accordance with that," but he looks back to their conversion as setting the tone for their Christian living.

Most Christians who look back on many years of Christian discipleship do detect a number of points at which God seemed to speak to them in a special way so that they were able to make a step forward in their Christian progress. When these stages of Christian growth are compared, one may stand out above the others, both in its depth and in the effect it has had on the person's life. But this does not mean that we have here a second experience which is the norm for every Christian.

Whenever God's Word challenges us, our response should be immediate and decisive. The aorist imperative is very often used in the New Testament to convey this sense of immediacy. Is there a sin to forsake? Then this calls for a definite act of repentance. So the Laodicean church was called to repent with an aorist imperative, although it was commanded to be zealous in the present imperative, which implies a continuing attitude (Rev 3:19). Jesus called for a decisive response in Matthew 5:30: "If your right hand causes you to sin, cut it off and throw it away." As James Philip realizes,

> That is crisis enough in the believer's experience, in that it demands drastic action to put matters right, just as, in the sphere of medicine, appendicitis is a "crisis" requiring immediate surgical intervention to safeguard life and health. But this drastic "crisis-action" in the spiritual realm is therapeutic, and in one very important sense only preparatory to the real business of Christian growth. It removes the hindrance to growth, and makes it possible, but it is not the growth itself, just as surgery removes the cause of illness, and makes possible better health in the future.[4]

God's Word often calls us to such a response. However, a word of caution is called for here. While the use of the aorist does imply a decisive step of obedience to God's Word, we have no right to build on this a doctrine of a once-for-all crisis of surrender subsequent to conversion. People sometimes cite the aorist tense used for "yield yourselves" in Romans 6:13 to make this point. They claim that this must refer to a single crisis point in the Christian life. If Christians want to live victoriously, they must at some time pass through this crisis.

If this system of interpretation is followed throughout the New Testament whenever an aorist imperative is encountered, some very curious theories could be produced! What, for example, are we to do with the succession of aorists in 2 Timothy 4:2, "Preach the word, be urgent in season and out of season, convince, rebuke and exhort"? The word *repent* is usually in the aorist tense in the New Testament, including Revelation 3:19 where it is addressed to church members. This, however, does not entitle us to teach a once-for-all crisis of repentance subsequent to conversion.[5] We have to decide from the context whether a once-for-all act is implied, and nothing in Romans 6 suggests that this is what Paul had in mind.

Perhaps an illustration will help at this point. I may say to my little boy, "Eat your vegetables." If I were speaking in the Greek of the New Testament, I might well use an aorist imperative because I want him to make a definite act of obedience. I would not, however, mean that this one act of obedience would be enough to last him the rest of his life! It is quite likely that whenever he is confronted with vegetables I will say the same thing in the same way. So it is with the command to yield in Romans 6. It does not say, "Yield yourselves to God and you will then live a life of constant victory." (There are verses in the New Testament where the aorist imperative is used in this way. Look, for example, at Acts 16:31, where there is a definite consequence following from a decisive act of faith.) But the meaning in Romans 6 is that whenever we are faced with a choice between yielding our members as "instruments of wickedness" or as "instruments of righteousness," we are to do the latter and to do it decisively.[6]

Some Examples of "Second Blessing"

What then are those experiences subsequent to conversion which seem to stand out above others? The following list is not exhaustive, but it gives some of those frequently encountered.

Recovery from backsliding. If conversion in the Bible means all that we have said about it, it is not surprising that some outstanding experiences in the Christian life are, in effect, a recovery of that first experience. Christians can backslide from what they possessed in Christ at conversion. James Philip has carefully interpreted the Scripture as it relates to this phenomenon.

According to the Scriptures, conversion and consecration are simultaneous, in the sense that no conversion ever really takes place that does not mean, imply and involve, a true consecration to Christ. One does not give part of one's allegiance to Christ at conversion, then at a later stage make a complete surrender to Him, called consecration. One does not enter into the kingdom at all except on terms of unconditional surrender.[7]

However, Christians can and often do fall away from the terms on which they started the Christian life, so James Philip continues:

A believer may lose the keen edge of his consecration and fall away from that attitude of total commitment which marked his entrance into the kingdom of God. If he does so, then a new consecration is necessary, and sometimes this is quite as clear-cut and decisive—and sudden—as a conversion experience, a crisis indeed, if this is the word to be used to describe it. But it is necessary to be clear about what has happened. It is not an advance to another stage of experience so much as a return to a previous one. A great deal depends on a true realization of this. For obviously, if a believer does not fall away from his first consecration, but follows on to know the Lord ever more deeply, he does not require to renew it again (except in so far as our consecration is renewed day by day, and hour by hour, which is not the point at issue here).

Discovering truth. Sometimes great blessings attend the rediscovery of a neglected truth. Didn't Paul experience this when God said to him, "My grace is sufficient for you" (2 Cor 12:9)? Many other Christians, too, have lived for years without a full realization of all that these words imply of the sufficiency of Christ.[8] Others have had what might be described as a "Calvinistic second blessing"! For many Christians look back warmly on their discovery of God's sovereignty and other truths connected with it. Verses like "You did not choose me, but I chose you" (Jn 15:16) have filled them with wonder at God's grace, that he should take the initiative in bringing them to a knowledge of salvation in Jesus Christ. They have come to realize that by nature they were dead in sin and utterly blind to the things of God, and that they would still be like that if God had not commanded the light of the gospel to shine into their darkened hearts (see 2 Cor 4:6). They now sing Charles Wesley's words with fresh understanding:

Long my imprisoned spirit lay
    Fast bound in sin and nature's night;
Thine eye diffused a quickening ray,—
    I woke, the dungeon flamed with light;
My chains fell off, my heart was free,
    I rose, went forth, and followed Thee.

An awareness of the cost of discipleship.   To live the Christian life is a costly matter. But Christians don't always face this fact right away. Many who have had the privilege of a Christian home have found it easy to make a Christian profession, perhaps less costly than resisting the gospel! Others may have entered the kingdom of God in a camp or house party for young people where everyone was professing conversion.

It was in circumstances like these that Jesus made a special point of emphasizing the cost of discipleship. "And there went great multitudes with him; and he turned, and said unto them," in essence, that discipleship was costly. Apparently Jesus saw the danger inherent in it becoming the fashion to follow him.

This important teaching is not always emphasized as it should be, and when stressed it still may not have the impact needed. For a time the young Christian may be oblivious to real stakes involved in following Christ. Then he or she goes out into the world, and there is a painful awakening. Living the Christian life is no longer the easy thing it was in the shelter of a Christian home, or perhaps in a school that upheld reasonable standards of decency. To be a Christian now involves going against the stream, being thought odd, and often being ridiculed for one's faith and the standard one seeks to maintain. This may have a chilling effect on the zeal of a Christian. The issues of discipleship have to be faced again, this time with the cost in view. Such an experience may precipitate a real crisis, the Christian must choose to step forward or backward. The former brings a blessing.

"Full assurance."　　There is a difference between a faith which is sufficient for salvation and faith which is sufficient for full assurance; and not every Christian has the latter. Hebrews 6:11 urges us to seek diligently "the full assurance of hope," and we are to approach God in prayer in that assurance (Heb 10:22). We are to use our Bibles to give us assurance: I write this to you . . . that you may know" (1 Jn 5:13). The same Epistle of John tells us many ways we can be sure of our place in Christ. Above all, it is the Holy Spirit himself who imparts the inward certainty to the heart of the believer.

> For you did not receive the spirit of slavery to fall back into fear, but you have received the spirit of sonship. When we cry, "Abba! Father!" it is the Spirit himself bearing witness with our spirit that we are children of God, and if children, then heirs, heirs of God and fellow heirs with Christ, provided we suffer with him in order that we may also be glorified with him. (Rom 8:15-17)

Now this can often come as an experience subsequent to conversion. It is not necessarily sudden in its effect, but it is nonetheless a clearly discernible step in the progress of a Christian. "Such a fact is constantly asserted by the saints throughout the centuries. They declare that the Holy Spirit made them so certain of the reality and presence of the Lord Jesus Christ and His love for them, that they were more certain of that than of any other fact whatsoever."[9]

An awareness of guidance.   A young person's discovery of God's will for his or her life, followed by the obedient response, can indeed be a decisive step with far-reaching effects in the quality of his or her life. Sometimes such a decision can follow a long period of conflict and struggle until a willingness to do God's will ensues. Jonah's experience was surely like this.

Special gifts of the Holy Spirit.   Christians sometimes claim to have an experience of the Holy Spirit which has led to their exercising special gifts, such as tongues. It is not within the scope of this book to assess these claims.[10] However, there is one relevant point to make here: such experiences do not have any *necessary*, *direct* connection with sanctification. Notice that I am choosing my words carefully, because the experiences we are here considering may have an important *indirect* effect on a person's holiness. For example, they may bring the believer assurance, which has a real bearing on the way a Christian lives. However, there is no *necessary* connection between the two.

We see a clear example of this in the Corinthian church. They were well endowed with gifts of the Holy Spirit, as Paul points out. "You are not lacking in any spiritual gift" (*charisma*; 1 Cor 1:7). Yet for all that, they had not for the most part progressed to any high degree of sanctification. In the third chapter he describes them as not spiritual, but carnal. Paul "makes it clear that the evidence of the Spirit's fullness is not the exercise of His gifts (of which they had plenty), but the ripening of His fruit (of which they had little)."[11] So Christians may possess a gift as high on the list in 1 Corinthians 12 as that of teaching—they may even be in great demand for speaking—and yet at the same time may have advanced little in holiness of life and in the fullness of the Spirit.

How shall we summarize this chapter? That Christians do have critical points in their lives that affect their future no one can deny. They can often be beneficial. What I have tried to do is to interpret them in the light of Scripture instead of vice versa. By doing so, we avoid the error of insisting that every Christian needs such an experience after conversion. Too, we can observe the way that these critical experiences vary. It brings home to us that all Christians are individuals who have been shaped by particular spiritual environments. The teaching we have received is always incomplete and often deficient. Some have not been warned of what it costs to be a Christian. Others have never realized that faith in Christ involves complete consecration to him, while others yet have never appreciated the sufficiency which is theirs in Christ. Perhaps they have not faced the true nature of sin and its seriousness. As a person progresses in the Christian life, these deficiencies are made up. A discovery may well bring sudden and dramatic results. So while the Christian life is normally presented in the New Testament as a steady growth, crises along the way may initiate decisive growth spurts in our sanctification.

11
The Fullness of the Holy Spirit

Certain believers claim that experiencing the "fullness of the Holy Spirit" has been for them a major impetus in their growth. And such claims are often connected with charismatic gifts. We must ask first, Is it fair to New Testament teaching to regard such a filling as an experience subsequent to conversion? And second, we ask the question integral to our theme: What does it have to do with holiness?

With one exception the occurrences of the phrase are confined to the writings of Luke. The first person described as filled with the Holy Spirit was John the Baptist—beginning "from his mother's womb" (Lk 1:15). Jesus also was said to be full of the Holy Spirit after he was baptized and as he went into the desert to be tempted (4:1). Luke gives us further examples in the early chapters of Acts. He begins with the Day of Pentecost, when the assembled company were all filled with the Holy Spirit (Acts 2:4), an event which was repeated later (4:31). Peter (4:8), Stephen (7:55) and Barnabas (11:24) are individuals marked as full of the Spirit. The effect was to enable them to "speak the word of God with boldness" (4:31); for Peter and Stephen this was in face of persecution. On the Day of Pentecost they were enabled "to speak in other tongues" languages which were recognized by visitors to Jerusalem (2:4, 11).

It is not easy to use these references for our present study because they have little, if anything, to say on the theme of holiness, except perhaps in the case of Barnabas, where his being filled with the Holy Spirit is closely linked to the fact that "he was a good man," "full . . . of faith." Besides, Luke's account tells us nothing about what these men had to do in order to become filled with the Spirit. The action is simply attributed to the hand of God. It happened to the infant church as they obeyed their Lord's command to "wait for the promise of the Father" (1:4). They waited, and the Father fulfilled the promise: he gave the Spirit. From here on, the filling by the Holy Spirit seems to have been the normal Christian experience. The apostles in Acts 6:3 assume that the seven who would take care of the Jerusalem widows would be "full of the Spirit" (6:3). Just as the company on the Day of Pentecost were all filled with the Holy Spirit, so were the new converts at Antioch in Pisidia (13:52).

So how does being filled with the Spirit relate to being holy? If Christians fall short of holiness, do they need a filling of the Spirit? To answer these questions we turn to the Epistles, where we find the only occurrence of this expression outside the writings of Luke. In Ephesians 5:18 we read the command "Be filled with the Spirit." A glance at the context establishes its relevance to our quest, for it is all about practical holiness.

No Separate Gospel of the Holy Spirit

We see immediately that the command is addressed to the ordinary Christian. This epistle is not directed only to the Christian leaders or those with special tasks to perform. Nor was it written to deal with any particular contingency which had arisen in the Ephesian church. This command is of relevance to every Christian. Why then is it found only here in this New Testament letter? What about the other churches to which Paul wrote? Didn't they too need to be filled with the Spirit? Paul was, for example, dealing with some heavy problems in the churches at Galatia, Colossae and Corinth. A filling of the Spirit would have gone a long way to meet their needs. Surely the Corinthians whom Paul "could not address as spiritual men" (1 Cor 3:1) needed it. Some today are very ready to disparage preachers who do not use this language frequently enough; what would they say about Paul? And what about other New Testament writers who never use the expression at all? Surely the omission can be explained. Whenever the writers call God's people to the life he intends for them, they are speaking of that very Spirit-filled life we are considering. But they do not confine themselves to a stereotyped language. Nor do they speak of the filling by the Spirit as a formula to be applied in every situation.

We must guard against one basic misunderstanding: the implication by some speakers and writers that there is a gospel of the Holy Spirit separate from the gospel of Jesus Christ. They put it like this. Christians may be truly converted and born again, but miss out on the Holy Spirit. They may have received the benefits resulting from Christ's death, such as forgiveness and eternal life, without having received the Holy Spirit. If someone objects that no one can be born again without the Spirit (Jn 3:1-8), then the theory can be modified: a person can be regenerated by the Holy Spirit without having received him *in his fullness.*

But the New Testament knows no such separation between Christ and the Holy Spirit. From the Day of Pentecost one gospel was proclaimed which promised both the forgiveness of sins and the gift of the Spirit (Acts 2:38). What scriptural ground is there for thinking that God will sometimes give one without the other? The example advanced is the case of the Samaritans in Acts 8:14-17. But it is the only incident of its kind, and it is clearly exceptional. Not only was this the first time after Pentecost that the gospel had been preached outside Jerusalem, but it was in the face of considerable prejudice against the Samaritans (e.g., Jn 4:9). There was danger that the Samaritan Christians might not be accepted into Christian fellowship and be thereby left to form a separate sect. So they were given what has been called a "Samaritan Pentecost" to confirm that they were genuine members of the Christian church. The more usual conclusion to be drawn when the Holy Spirit is absent we find in Acts 19:1-7. Paul discovered certain disciples who had not even heard of the Holy Spirit. Far from calling them to a second blessing, he questioned whether they were Christians at all; he asked about their baptism. On learning that they had not gone beyond the discipleship of John the Baptist, he told them about Jesus, and they then received Christian baptism for the first time. The filling of the Spirit came with it.

What the Acts demonstrates by its record of preaching and events, the Epistles assert doctrinally. We have seen in Ephesians 1 how God has given us all his blessings in Christ. He has "blessed in Christ with *every spiritual* blessing" (Eph 1:3), and what are "spiritual blessings" if not those of the Holy Spirit? Paul expands this thought in the following verses: salvation is ours because we were chosen and destined for it by the Father (vv. 4-6), because we have been redeemed by the blood of Christ (vv. 7-12), and because we have the Holy Spirit as the seal and guarantee (vv. 13-14). With work of the Holy Spirit set in the triad of the Trinity, we know that we are considering one of the basic doctrines of the Christian faith. It affects, too, our understanding of the person of Christ and his full deity.

Paul's Epistle to the Colossians clarifies this doctrine as it relates to our question. The Colossian Christians were in danger of undervaluing our Lord's person, and so Paul declared to them that "in him the whole fullness of deity dwells" (Col 2:9). The older version renders *deity* as "the Godhead," making it even clearer that the entire Godhead, including the Holy Spirit, is in Christ. With irresistible logic follows the next verse: "And you have come to fullness of life in him." So if we possess Christ we have been given everything that God has for us, including the Holy Spirit *in his fullness*. The command in Ephesians 5:8 cannot be to seek something in addition to what we already have in Christ.

Christ and the Holy Spirit are sometimes referred to interchangeably. Jesus does it himself when he teaches on this subject in John 14—16. Of the Holy Spirit he says, "He will be in you" (14:17); in the following verse the wording becomes "I will come to you." A few verses later the Father is included. "If a man loves me, he will keep my word, and my Father will love him, and *we* will come to him and make our abode with him" (v. 23). Paul speaks in the same way where within one verse he calls the Holy Spirit "the Spirit," "the Spirit of God" and "the Spirit of Christ" (Rom 9:8). This does not imply that the three persons are indistinguishable. Each has his distinct ministry. But they always work together, and we cannot have one without the others. Although Christ has ascended into heaven and his bodily presence has been withdrawn from the earth, he is still able to indwell the hearts of his people. He does it by his Holy Spirit.

Some people account for spiritual shortcomings by separating, as a time sequence, the work of Christ from the work of the Spirit. They assume that the failing Christian is spiritually in the gap that the disciples experienced historically between the death of Christ and Pentecost. If the historical separation of the two events is taken as a normative pattern for Christians, new believers should experience redemption and then wait—wait, seeking as the disciples did for the separate gift of the Spirit.

But Jesus had already said that those who come to him would receive the Holy Spirit in abundance (Jn 7:37-39). The disciples had most certainly come to him, so why were they still waiting for the gift of the Holy Spirit? Had their response been defective, that they had received only part of what Jesus wanted to give them? The Gospel writer supplies in the same text the explanation. "As yet the Holy Spirit had not been given, because Jesus was not yet glorified." When that glorifying of Jesus had been completed by his death, resurrection and ascension, within a few days the Holy Spirit was poured out in abundance. In other words, they were in their waiting condition simply because the Pentecost event had not yet taken place. But ever since Pentecost the promise of Jesus has operated, so that those who come to him receive not only forgiveness of sins but also the Holy Spirit in full measure. Paul can therefore assert that in Christ we have every spiritual blessing. To compare true Christians who are in Christ to the disciples before Pentecost is as misleading as it would be to place a Christian today between Good Friday and Easter, blessed by the death of Christ but not by his resurrection.

Finally, some theorize that we can receive the Holy Spirit for the new birth—but not in abundance. This view coincides with the separation between justification and sanctification which we examined in chapter seven and discovered to be contrary to Scripture. It is likewise contrary to Scripture to divide the work of the Holy Spirit. In the promise of the Holy Spirit in John 7:37-39 Jesus makes no such distinction. Those who come to him receive the Holy Spirit in measure like flowing rivers. When Scripture calls Christians to appreciate their blessings and to live up to the standard of life that God expects of them, it always points back to their conversion or baptism, never to some later experience (e.g., Col 2:6-7; Rom 6:3).

A Command to Obey

Since God has already "blessed us in Christ with every spiritual blessing," Paul presents the fullness of the Holy Spirit not as a further experience to seek, but as a command to obey. "Be filled with the Spirit." It is, as John Stott has put it,

> not a tentative suggestion, a mild recommendation, a polite piece of advice. It is a command which comes to us from Christ with all the authority of one of his chosen apostles. We have no more liberty to escape this duty than we have the ethical duties which surround the text, e.g. to speak the truth, to do honest work, to be kind and forgiving to one another, or to live lives of purity and love. The fullness of the Holy Spirit is not optional for the Christian, but obligatory.[1]

The tense here is a *present* imperative, which denotes not a single action, as does the aorist, but a continuous one. Paul is not presenting us with a response which we make once for all, but with an attitude to maintain day by day throughout our lives. This command is for something much more than a spurt in our growth.

It is grammatically significant that the verb is passive. But how does one obey a passive command? To be told "Touch that person" is simple enough, but what about "Be touched by that person"? Such a command assumes that the other person is trying to touch us, and we are being asked to allow him to do so. Paul's language is a very fitting way of describing what we must do with the Holy Spirit who came to fill us at our conversion—we are commanded to allow him to do so. Well does the New English Bible render the command, "Let the Holy Spirit fill you." If we fail to progress in the way of holiness, we may not only be doing the things we ought not to, but we may be thwarting the Holy Spirit from having his way with us.

Elsewhere Paul has two other ways of expressing the same command. In Ephesians we are told, "Do not grieve the Holy Spirit of God" (4:30). The Holy Spirit is a person with whom we enjoy an intimate relationship; if we indulge in unholy living, against which Paul has been warning his readers, we impair that relationship. The command "Do not quench the Spirit" (1 Thess 5:19) likens him to fire which can be dampened by carnal behavior.

The Spirit and the Word

Just what is the Holy Spirit trying to do? If this were a book on practical living, we would start by turning to the fruit of the Spirit listed in Galatians 5:22-23. But we are engaged here in a doctrinal study of *how* the Holy Spirit brings about our sanctification with all its fruits, which is the goal of a Christian. So let us refer instead to the parallel passage in the letter to the Colossians where we find an important feature of his work.

When we put the two letters side by side, we see that Paul must have written them at about the same time. They are similar not only in subject matter but in language, which in many places is almost identical. Colossians 3 holds the passage parallel to Ephesians 5. For the command to be filled with the Spirit, in Colossians Paul makes an interesting substitution. For it he writes, "Let the word of Christ dwell in you richly" (3:16). Apparently Paul thinks of Spirit and Word interchangeably, and a person who is filled by the Spirit is presumably filled also by his Word—and vice versa.

This close connection between Spirit and Word exists all through Scripture. It is not a novel idea introduced by Paul. In the first few verses of the Bible we read that "the Spirit of God was moving over the face of the waters. And God said . . ." (Gen 1:2-3). The psalmist attributes this work of creation to both Word and Spirit: "By the word of the LORD the heavens were made, and all their hosts by the *breath* [this is the same word as *spirit* in Hebrew and Greek] of his mouth" (Ps 33:6). The close relationship between God's Spirit and his Word is seen too in the inspiration of the Scriptures. "All scripture," declared Paul, "is inspired by God" (2 Tim 3:16), which means literally that it is "God-breathed."

Our particular interest is, however, in the way that Spirit and Word are involved together in the work of sanctification. It begins with regeneration when we are born again by God's Spirit.[2] At that stage the Word of God is also involved: "You have been born anew," writes Peter, "not of perishable seed but of imperishable, through the living and abiding word of God" (1 Pet 1:23; cf. Jas 1:18). The work of sanctification proceeds as the Holy Spirit applies God's Word to our hearts and lives.

Two Old Testament prophets foresaw the mark of the Spirit in human lives as the distinctive of the new covenant. Ezekiel looks for the day when God will "put a new spirit within them." Whether this should be spelled with a small or capital "s," a new spirit can be produced in a person only by the Holy Spirit. The new spirit will make a difference in their lives such that they will "walk in my statutes and keep my ordinances and obey them" (Ezek 11:19-20 and cf. 36:26-27). What does the work of the Holy Spirit within God's people have to do with their obedience to God's Word? Jeremiah answers, "I will put my law within them, and I will write it upon their hearts" (Jer 31:33). Paul must have had both these references in mind when he described his readers as "a letter from Christ delivered by us, written not with ink but with the Spirit of the living God, not on tablets of stone but on tablets of human hearts" (2 Cor 3:3). So, as we saw in the latter part of chapter five, we are sanctified not only by the Holy Spirit but by the Word of God which he writes on our hearts.

Christians who let the Holy Spirit fill them will be diligent in their use of the Bible. They will constantly expose themselves to its teaching and allow it to shape their outlooks and personalities. Their behavior will increasingly conform to the standards of God revealed in Scripture. The Word of God will, in short, be the test and interpreter of all their experiences. Sadly, not all of those who *claim* to be filled with the Spirit are governed by this principle. Because they make themselves and their feelings the main criteria for what they regard as true, their yardstick is all too often "what I find helpful." The Holy Spirit, however, does not fill us to pander to our feelings but rather to impose God's living Word upon us so that we are recreated in his image.

Our progress with the Word of God then, is one of the chief signs of our spiritual maturity. The Corinthians, for all their fascination with charismatic gifts, Paul regarded not as "spiritual men, but as men of the flesh, as babes in Christ." He says, "I fed you with milk, not solid food; for you were not ready for it; and even now you are not ready" (1 Cor 3:1-2; cf. Heb 5:11-14). Those whose main spiritual diet never progresses beyond trivial, repetitive phrases set to tune ought to ask themselves some serious questions.

The Marks of the Spirit's Fullness

Diligence with the Word of God demands that we use our minds both to understand and to apply it. Paul says, "I of myself serve the law of God with my mind" (Rom 7:25). And it is the mind of a Christian which he emphasizes in the verses just before the command to be filled with the Spirit. We are to live "carefully," being "wise," and we are to "understand" God's will (Eph 5:15, 17). The Holy Spirit works through a person's mind because it controls his life—his choices and actions.

As the mind controls the person, so the Spirit wants charge of the mind. Hence the contrast in Ephesians 5:18 between being filled by the Spirit and being drunk, with one's mind impaired. Some have maintained that Paul is not making a contrast here but a comparison, that he is regarding the fullness of the Spirit as a kind of spiritual intoxication producing a state of stupor. They can thereby defend the excesses which sometimes occur. It is, however, an impossible interpretation. Although on the Day of Pentecost some people in the Jerusalem crowd did say of the disciples that they were filled with new wine (Acts 2:13), it was an unfair comment based on ignorance, as John Stott has explained.

> Those who said this were evidently a minority who supposed the disciples to be drunk because they could not understand any of the languages spoken, whereas the reaction of the majority was astonishment that the Galilean disciples were speaking intelligibly in the native languages of Asia and Africa which the crowd could understand.[3]

Since Paul is stressing how a Christian's mind needs to be in control of his or her life, it can hardly be compared to the drunken state in which one is out of control. D. Martyn Lloyd-Jones reminds us that alcohol is not a stimulant, as it is popularly described, but a depressant.

> It knocks out those higher centers and so the more primitive elements in the brain come up and take control; and a man feels better temporarily. He has lost his sense of fear, and he has lost his discrimination, he has lost his power to assess. Alcohol merely knocks out his higher centers and releases the more instinctive, primal elements; but the man believes that he is being stimulated. What is really true of him is that he has become more of an animal; his control over himself is diminished.[4]

How utterly different is the effect of the Holy Spirit! "He really does stimulate," Lloyd-Jones continues. He stimulates every faculty—intellect, heart and will. A controlled life with the mind alert: this is what Paul enjoins for the Christian in Ephesians 5.

The apostle chooses three key areas which the mind of a Spirit-filled Christian will control. The first is the general way we live. "Look carefully then how you walk," writes Paul, using one of his favorite metaphors for the Christian life, "not as unwise men but as wise" (v. 15). "Look carefully *then*" implies that we should give constant attention to the ways in which our behavior must differ from the pagan life-style Paul has been describing in verses 3-14.

Second, our thought must control our use of time, as this will largely determine what we achieve with our lives. We use a number of verbs commonly with the word *time*. We can *spend* time, *make* time or *save* time. The Bible speaks of *redeeming* time, a word rich with doctrinal associations, because time needs to be delivered from its bondage to evil (v. 16). Paul's choice of words contains a further idea. Of the two common Greek words for time he uses the one meaning "season" or "opportunity." So the Revised Standard Version has good reason for the rendering "making the most of the time," as has the New International Version with "making the most of every opportunity." Spirit-filled Christians will be disciplined in planning their time, and their discipline will underscore another contrast to drunkenness. The word translated "debauchery" in verse 18 is the word for "save" with a negative prefix; it means "waste" or "squander." Luke 15 uses the word to describe the riotous living of the prodigal son. Drunkenness squanders time, money, dignity and many human potentialities. The Holy Spirit, on the other hand, conserves all that is best and produces a life which, instead of being dissipated, is productive.

Third, our minds are to discover God's will with a view to making right decisions. "Do not be foolish (Gk., 'without reason')," advises Paul in this matter (v. 17). A common type of foolishness is overreliance on feelings and inner promptings, which result in glibly made claims such as "The Lord told me" and "I feel led." While it may be nothing more than an immature phase through which many of us pass, it can be damaging, especially when accompanied by arrogance. Relying on feelings is far removed from using God-given wisdom which is "open to reason" (Jas 3:17). History contains notorious examples of movements dominated by leaders claiming special revelations. J. I. Packer has written of them, "Their basic mistake is to think of guidance as essentially inward prompting by the Holy Spirit, apart from the written Word. This idea, which is as old as the false prophets of the Old Testament... is a seed-bed in which all forms of fanaticism and folly can grow."[5]

Paul's method of guidance is not to *feel* what the will of the Lord is but to *understand,* and normally the New Testament leaders made decisions by their understanding. Now we do find isolated examples of visions and inner promptings, but these were exceptions rather than the norm. The second and third missionary journeys began because the new converts needed help (Acts 15:36; 18:20-23). Paul stayed on in Ephesus because of the opportunities there (1 Cor 16:8-9). He decided to send Timothy to Philippi based on his assessment of him and his desire to learn about the Philippian church (Phil 2:19-24). The term *sanctified common sense* may have become a cliché, but it still has meaning. Is not our common sense being sanctified as the Holy Spirit shapes our minds by God's Word, so that we naturally make our decisions according to God's will? Paul calls it "the renewal of your mind," which has as its purpose "that you may prove what is the will of God, what is good and acceptable and perfect" (Rom 12:2).

So much then for what Paul says just before the command to be filled with the Spirit. The verses that follow have a very different emphasis. By a series of participles dependent on the command, he sets out the result of being filled—the psalms and hymns and spiritual songs of Christian worship. Here enter the feelings and emotions. Clearly Paul has suggested a balance which not everyone maintains. As Bernard Mobbs observed, "To some people religion is a perpetual debate, to others an emotional orgy."[6] Neither extreme will do. If it is all in the mind, our Christianity will be lifeless, insipid. Without mind and understanding it will be an empty effervescence. The Anglican collect for Whitsunday preserves the balance when it says, "Grant us by the same Spirit to have a right judgment in all things, and evermore to rejoice . . ."

It is relevant to our study of Christian growth to note the worship that goes along with the Spirit's filling. First, it is manward in that we are "addressing one another" (v. 19). We need both to give encouragement and to receive it from one another, "not neglecting to meet together, as is the habit of some, but encouraging one another" (Heb 10:25). In the "fellowship of the Holy Spirit" we grow in holiness. Spiritual worship is also Godward, "singing and making melody *to the Lord.*" More than just enjoying the feelings aroused by a sentimental tune, we express in song the God-centeredness which is essential to true holiness. The phrase "with all your heart" affirms the believers' wholehearted involvement. And thankfulness in everything (v. 20) marks the Spirit-filled believer now just as it marked the Old Testament worshiper in the Temple.

A very practical section, dealing with relationships in marriage and the family and also at work, follows Paul's command to be filled with the Spirit. He introduces it with the call to "be subject to one another" (v. 21). Mutual submission is not only one of the secrets of happy relationships, but it is also a direct result of being filled with the Spirit. This is somewhat obscured by translating it as a fresh command, but it is, in fact, the fourth participle depending on "be filled with the Spirit." Self-assertion is much encouraged in the world, but it can never be a characteristic of those who are filled with the Spirit, since they will be motivated by their reverence for Christ. "The Holy Spirit is a humble Spirit, and those who are truly filled with him always display the meekness and gentleness of Christ."[7]

We now return to the question with which this chapter began: Does the fullness of the Holy Spirit involve an event subsequent to conversion? Yes, it can. When Christians are convicted of how far they are falling short of the blessings which are theirs in Christ, they may well return to what they had received at their conversion with a repentance which is clear and decisive. Indeed, the apostle John once challenged the church at Ephesus in this very way: "Remember then from what you have fallen, repent and do the works you did at first" (Rev 2:5).

At the same time we must recognize that the command to be filled with the Spirit is to a continuous, daily appropriation rather than to a once-for-all response. As with the life of growth described in chapter nine, through an increasing knowledge, faith and love we appropriate more and more of the blessings God has made ours in Christ. As we grow in grace our capacity will increase, even as a baby's lungs develop with age.

Christians who are filled with the Spirit will live ordered, disciplined lives controlled by their minds, which are in turn submitted to God's Word. Sanctification and the Word of God are deeply linked, as we saw in the last part of chapter five. The fullness of the Holy Spirit then has more to do with holiness of life than with charismatic gifts. He is after all the *Holy* Spirit![8]

12
Faith
and
Effort

We know that God is working in us to make us holy. What are *we* supposed to do? What part do we people play in the sanctifying process? Traditionally the church has answered with two voices. One says we are involved by faith, the other by effort. The first says we surrender; the second says we strive. These two polar emphases are respectively denoted by the terms *quietism* and *pietism*.

Quietism
Quietism, a rather mystical view, was originally popular among the Quakers, but it has been adopted by some of the forms of perfectionism noted in chapter eight. The work of sanctification, says the quietist, involves no effort on our

part. Indeed, our striving and effort can even hinder our sanctification. Our part is simply to surrender ourselves to God and to let him give us victory over sin. The surrender usually comes at a crucial point subsequent to conversion, although the believer must maintain it as a daily attitude. While we are in this attitude of surrender, we live victoriously. We fall into sin only when we cease to trust him completely. Words like yield, surrender and abandonment recur frequently, as does the catchy saying "Let go, and let God."[1] Two lines of a hymn express it simply:

Holiness by faith in Jesus,
    Not by effort of my own.

These lines clearly imply that the Christian has to choose between faith and effort, and the way of holiness is to choose faith.

This teaching has led to some extreme conclusions. For example, Galatians 2:20—especially the phrase *Not I, but Christ*—is taken out of its context to suggest that a Christian's personality is to be virtually obliterated and replaced by Christ's. Expressions like *yield yourselves* (Rom 8:13) are taken to recommend a state of passive surrender to God in which we need ourselves offer no resistance to temptation; we should simply leave it to God to give us the victory. Some have even claimed that Christians in this state of yieldedness do not experience temptation because he defeats it before they can! Some writers have devoted a remarkable amount of space to explaining what they mean by *surrender* and other words in their terminology. If these words represent biblical concepts, one would expect a little more attention given to them in the Bible itself.

A Major Objection
Quite apart from such extremes, the whole theory embraces a major difficulty which has never really been answered. Who is at fault when a Christian sins? (The supporters of

this view usually admit that there is such a possibility.)
Whose fault is the failure? It is hardly the Christian's fault
because when he or she surrenders to God, God then assumes responsibility. Yet we shrink from any suggestion
that the fault may lie with God himself. One answer is that
Christians sin only because they have ceased to trust, because they have left the position of self-surrender, by which
they had placed themselves completely in the hands of God.
But this does not answer the difficulty at all, for ceasing to
trust in God is in itself a sin. We are still left with the question, Whose fault is it that the Christian has ceased to trust?
How can Christians who have handed their lives over to God
ever sin again?

Faced with tough objections, quietists draw heavily on
analogy for help—not the best hermeneutical principle.
Pearsall Smith chooses the biblical analogy of the potter and
the clay, but her use of it goes far beyond what we find in
Jeremiah. She begins,

> What can be said about man's part in this great work, but
> that he must continually surrender himself and continually
> trust? But when we come to God's side of the question,
> what is there that may not be said as to the manifold and
> wonderful ways in which He accomplishes the work en-
> trusted to Him? It is here that the growing comes in. The
> lump of clay could never grow into a beautiful vessel if it
> stayed in the clay-pit for thousands of years; but when it
> is put into the hands of a skilful potter it grows rapidly,
> under his fashioning, into the vessel he intends it to be.
> And in the same way the soul, abandoned to the working
> of the Heavenly Potter, is made into a vessel unto honour,
> sanctified, and meet for the Master's use.[2]

Why then do things go wrong? Here is how Pearsall Smith
accounts for the failure of a lady who had "lost all her blessing": "She had understood her part of trusting to begin with,
but, not understanding the Divine process of accomplish-

ing that for which she had trusted, she took herself out of the hands of the Heavenly Potter, and the vessel was marred on the wheel."[3] One moment a Christian is like a piece of malleable clay, soft and without any will of its own, and the next moment like a piece of clay that decides to jump out of the potter's hand. Some clay!

Much as we realize the inadequacies of the quietist point of view, we must have some sympathy with its genuine attempt to stress that salvation is of the Lord. It has tried to show that people are as incapable of sanctifying themselves as they are of justifying themselves. And it has rightly recognized that what God has done for us in Christ for our sanctification is as sufficient as any other aspect of his salvation. "I can't, Christ can" they will say. With these premises we must agree. But the quietist viewpoint moves from here to the untenable conclusion that all Christians can do is passively let God do everything. While they allow him, the work of sanctification will proceed and they will live the victorious Christian life. Everything depends on Christians maintaining a state of surrender to Christ and abiding in him. Here the whole theory fails in what it set out to do; sanctification depends not on God at all but on people and their maintaining of surrender; not on the potter but on the clay.

A second drawback to this teaching is that it produces a uniformity of personality. As Lloyd-Jones has pointed out, "If we are to do nothing but just give in and not exert ourselves and our powers, obviously we shall all conform to a certain type and to a certain pattern—the difference between Peter and Paul and John and James will vanish, and Calvin and Luther and Bunyan, and Jonathan Edwards and George Whitefield will become identical in the common absence of certain things from their lives."[4]

The Place of Effort

To pit faith against effort is a false antithesis, one never made in Scripture. *Of course* faith is necessary in sanctification. The depth of our faith bears directly on the extent of our growth (see chapter nine). But this does not preclude effort. People who are being renewed by the Holy Spirit are not in a state of passive surrender. They are actively engaged in mortifying the flesh and in putting on the new creation (see chapter fourteen). The Christian life is described as a race (Heb 12:1), and as a fight (Eph 6:10-18; 1 Tim 6:12); both analogies definitely imply effort on the part of the Christian. We have to be careful to apply ourselves to good deeds (Tit 3:8).

The devil is an enemy to be resisted (Jas 4:7). Paul finds it necessary to pommel his body and subdue it lest he be disqualified (1 Cor 9:27).[5] Quietists call up the strong appeal of the "rest of faith" in Hebrews 3 and 4, and, of course, God intends us to know his rest increasingly in our lives; but notice the paradox: "Let us therefore strive to enter that rest" (Heb 4:11).

If all a Christian needs to do is simply remain passive like a piece of clay in a potter's hands, then it is hard to see the reason for the practical teachings in the New Testament. If we are supposed just to let Christ "live out his life in us," why are there such injunctions as "Look carefully then how you walk" (Eph 5:15)? And what about Paul's description of his own life: "I press on toward the goal" (Phil 3:14)? Remember that the verb here is a word used of an athlete straining every nerve to win. The New Testament motivates us to greater effort toward holiness. "Since we have these promises, beloved," writes the apostle, "let us cleanse ourselves from every defilement of body and spirit, and make holiness perfect in the fear of God" (2 Cor 7:1). No, there are no short cuts to victory in the New Testament, no secret formulas to be discovered. Rather, we need to submit to the whole range of teaching in the Word of God if we are to make progress in sanctification. Holiness does not come in a moment, but as the hymn expresses it, we must "take time to be holy."

Pietism

The word *pietism* is not as self-descriptive as *quietism* in explaining its view of sanctification. The name comes from the movement in eighteenth-century Germany which protested the dead orthodoxy of the Lutheran church at the time. It encouraged much that was good, such as the growth of Bible study groups. Primarily it called for a practical Christianity, emphasizing the uselessness of belief which does not lead to good works. The word *pietism* represents for theologians an emphasis on diligence in practical Christianity and an insistence on self-discipline and spiritual exercises.

Discernible in pietism is a danger every bit as harmful as that in unbalanced quietism. With an overemphasis on effort a Christian could easily forget that it is God who sanctifies and that we must rest trusting on God and all his promises. Pietists are inevitably trapped by the result of their efforts. If they fail they may well suffer despair, while if they succeed they may succumb to self-congratulation instead of glorifying God. God has indeed given us everything in Christ, but this does not mean that after his initial saving he leaves people to purify themselves. When we are told to work out our own salvation, we are immediately assured that God works in us (Phil 2:12-13); the word *works* is in the present tense. Stressing the importance of practical Christianity, we declare with James, "Faith by itself, if it has no works, is dead" (Jas 2:17). But at the same time, "without faith it is impossible to please him" (Heb 11:6).

Maintaining the Balance

We have juxtaposed here two sets of complementary truths, and we err in neglecting either side. The balance is carefully maintained in Scripture. For example, in 2 Peter 1:3-4 the apostle emphasizes all that God has done for us to guarantee our sanctification: "His divine power has granted to us all things that pertain to life and godliness, through the knowledge of him who called us to his own glory and excellence, by which he has granted to us his precious and very great promises, that through these you may escape from the corruption that is in the world because of passion, and become partakers of the divine nature." However, it does not end there. Peter goes on to list virtues over which the Christian must show diligence. He says in verses 5-9,

> For this very reason make every *effort* to supplement your *faith* with virtue, and virtue with knowledge, and knowledge with self-control, and self-control with steadfastness, and steadfastness with godliness, and godliness with brotherly affection, and brotherly affection with love. For if these things are yours and abound, they keep you from being ineffective or unfruitful in the knowledge of our Lord Jesus Christ. For whoever lacks these things is blind and shortsighted and has forgotten that he was cleansed from his old sins.

Verse 10 tells one result of such diligence: the Christian makes his or her "calling and election sure" (KJV).

How can sanctification still be the work of God when the Christian has to be so active in the pursuit of it? Surely the answer comes in words we have already quoted: "God is at work in you, both to will and to work for his good pleasure" (Phil 2:13). Christians are active because God stimulates us to effort and diligence, and he impresses on our conscience the encouragements and warnings of Scripture. So people who truly believe the gospel with all its provisions for our need and who look to Jesus, "the pioneer and perfecter of our faith," will be challenged to "run with perseverance the race that is set before us" (Heb 12:1-2). The paradox is one we continually face in the Christian life. We must continue with effort, but effort based on confidence in the sufficiency of Jesus Christ.

Fight the good fight with all thy might;
Christ is thy strength, and Christ thy right.

Incentives

We saw in chapter two that the holiness of God is the great stimulus to Christian holy living. The command "You shall be holy" is enforced by the sublime truth "I am holy." We find comparable incentives linking practice to doctrine in the Epistles. The reader gazes in chapters 1—3 of Ephesians at the great panorama of Christian truth and all the blessing of the gospel that belong to us in Christ. The remaining three chapters deal with practical matters based on those doctrines. Ephesians 4:1, as the connecting verse between the two portions of the book, calls us to right living: "I therefore, a prisoner for the Lord, beg you to lead a life worthy of the calling to which you have been called."

So faith and effort are intrinsically linked in Scripture in promoting holiness through incentives. It is not that secret formulas or easy short cuts bypassing effort are whispered into our ears, but rather that incentives stir us to endeavor in every part of our Christian lives.

And the incentive that stands above all others for the Christian is the very life of Christ. We are to follow his example. When Paul describes to the Philippians the characteristics that should mark their corporate life, he naturally thinks of Christ on his way to the cross. Christ was willing to be humiliated, and he remains for us an example of the lowliness of mind we should display toward each other (Phil 2:5-8). Peter also looks to Christ's example to show how a Christian should react when he or she is unjustly treated (1 Pet 2:18-25).

Incentives depend for their constraining or compelling power on the extent to which they are believed. The stronger the faith by which they are held, the stronger their compulsion on a Christian's life. For example, the stronger our faith in the humiliated Christ, the more we are compelled to act in humility toward one another. The deeper our faith in the Christ who crossed all kinds of barriers to love outcasts, the more we are strengthened to do the same. Effort that issues from such faith reinforces that faith. So when a Christian grows, his or her faith also grows.[6] "We have the same spirit of faith," Paul writes, "as he had who wrote, 'I believed, and so I spoke' " (2 Cor 4:13). Notice again the title of this chapter. It is not "Faith or Effort?" but "Faith *and* Effort"—inseparably.

13
The
Christian's
Enemies

The *Christian life is a fight.* We find in the Word of God a clear pattern of the life that God wants us to live, but opposing forces constantly draw us in the opposite direction. While on the one hand we strive to follow the example of our Master, a power seems always to be dragging us down; and again and again we perform actions, speak words and think thoughts that afterward we regret and are even ashamed of. We should not be surprised that the Christian life is like this. The Bible has warned us that it will be so. But we who are "following after holiness" will rally to the call of the Captain: "Fight the good fight of the faith" (1 Tim 6:12). We wrestle "against the spiritual hosts of wickedness in the heavenly places" (Eph 6:12).

If we want to be victorious in this conflict, we must first of all learn all we can about the enemy, and, as we might expect, the Bible gives us plenty of information. We discover that the enemy is threefold and usually denoted by the familiar trinity, "the world, the flesh and the devil."

The Devil

The ultimate enemy with which we have to reckon is the devil, and the Bible never underestimates his formidable nature and intention. The thief who "comes only to steal and kill and destroy" (Jn 10:10), his aim is nothing short of our complete destruction and ruin. He is given a variety of names in Scripture, such as "Satan" (which means literally "the adversary"), "the evil one" and "the god of this world" (2 Cor 4:4), to mention just a few. Speaking of his strength, the Bible likens him to a roaring lion who "prowls around . . . seeking some one to devour" (1 Pet 5:8). It is from the power of Satan that we need to be delivered (Acts 26:18).

However, we are confronted not only by devilish power, but also by a subtle, scheming mind behind that power. The Bible in another picture likens him to a serpent who is "more subtle than any other wild creature" (Gen 3:1). He "deceived Eve by his cunning" (2 Cor 11:3). He employs "designs" (2 Cor 2:11) and "wiles" (Eph 6:11—a word which Moffatt translates "stratagems"). Indeed the Bible represents him as the supreme example of a depraved mind. He is, as our Lord said, the father of falsehood (Jn 8:44). He can use people for his ends (e.g., Acts 13:10) and can even fill the heart of a professed believer (Acts 5:3). His masterstroke is to disguise himself as an angel of light (2 Cor 11:14).

Because of the devil's universal activity, temptation is "common to man" (1 Cor 10:13). No Christian is exempt. Even those (perhaps *especially* those) who have advanced furthest in holiness are objects of the devil's attentions. Because Jesus was a real man, he lay himself open to temptation, and the Gospels record his experience of it. So we need not feel guilty when we are tempted. It becomes sinful only when we nurture temptation and yield to it.

Nevertheless, the devil's power is not unlimited. We have a very telling picture in the first chapter of Job, where the curtain is drawn aside and we are given a glimpse into heaven at the eternal realities lying behind the conflicts of this world. Here we see Satan having to get God's permission before he can go and tempt Job. Paul also tells us that God limits the temptations to which a Christian is subjected (1 Cor 10:13). Satan has already been defeated by Jesus and his ultimate destruction is sure and certain. Every time the gospel is preached in power, we are assured of his ultimate fate (Lk 10:18-19), that "the God of peace will soon crush Satan under your feet" (Rom 16:20).

The witness of the New Testament then is clear. Satan is a malignant reality, always hostile to God and to God's people. But he has already been defeated in Christ's life and death and resurrection, and this defeat will become obvious and complete in the end of the age.[1]

The World
The devil takes hold of two positions familiar to us as sources of temptation: the world and the flesh. The devil is described as the god of this world (2 Cor 4:4) and the ruler of this world (Jn 12:31; 14:30; 16:11). In offering Christ all the kingdoms of this world, the devil assumed that they belonged to him already (Mt 4:8-9). The Bible always speaks of the world in its present condition as being temporarily occupied by the enemy. "We know," writes John, " . . . the whole world is in the power of the evil one" (1 Jn 5:19). This world is opposed to God, and it is out of it that Jesus came to redeem God's people.

We must carefully distinguish the world as I have just described it from the earth as God created it. About the latter there is nothing evil. "The earth is the LORD's and the fulness thereof" (Ps 24:1). Hence Paul rejects false asceticism, regarding it as a departure from the faith, "for everything created by God is good, and nothing is to be rejected if it is received with thanksgiving" (1 Tim 4:4). The world of human affairs, however, has been corrupted by sin, and as far as a Christian is concerned, it is an alien environment.

The Christian will relate to the world through his or her consecration. Jesus prayed for his disciples in the world, saying, "Sanctify them in the truth" (Jn 17:14-18). He states in John 17 the basic principle that Christians are to be "in the world, but not of the world." Here are two complementary truths about Christian living that we have to keep in balance. We see them both in the different uses of *Jerusalem* in two well-known hymns. One, a medieval hymn by Bernard of Cluny, was translated by J. M. Neale during the last century into the words "Jerusalem the golden." This Jerusalem is certainly not of this world nor in it. But William Blake's Jerusalem is very much in this world. He observed the "dark Satanic mills" of the Industrial Revolution and called for his bow of burning gold, his arrows of desire and his chariot of fire, resolving,

I will not cease from mental fight,
Nor shall my sword sleep in my hand,
Till we have built Jerusalem
In England's green and pleasant land.

In the world.   Jesus prayed for his disciples: "I do not pray that thou shouldst take them out of the world" (Jn 17:15), for it is in the world that a Christian is to witness for Jesus Christ and to live life. It is in the world that a Christian is to be salt and a light that shines before men (Mt 5:13-16).

Some Christians imagine that they can keep pure by living withdrawn from the world and its problems. Many of the great saints of God, whose lives are recorded in the pages of Scripture, expressed the desire to be taken out of the world, including such illustrious men as David, Moses, Elijah and Jonah. In no case, however, did God grant the request; instead he gave them special strength to endure the circumstances which provoked their feelings. If we imagine that by monastic withdrawal we can avoid sin, we shall be disillusioned. The medieval monasteries bear witness to this. Thomas à Kempis was prompted to write: "There is no order so holy, no place so secret, where there will be no temptation." In any case, God calls his people to be witnesses here in the world, in the very midst of evil: to exhibit the power of grace, to show forth faith, courage and patience as good soldiers of Jesus Christ. We are called to be like Daniel in Babylon and the saints in Caesar's household.

Of course, the supreme reason for a Christian remaining in the world and facing his responsibilities there is that by doing so he is following the example of Jesus. Jesus prayed, "As thou didst send me into the world, so I have sent them into the world" (Jn 17:18). He was "the Word become flesh" who "dwelt among us" (Jn 1:14); he mingled with people. He became known as the friend of publicans and sinners. He offended current ideas of separation even to the extent of being misunderstood and described as a glutton and a drunkard (Mt 11:19). And his was no inverted snobbery, for he mixed with the Pharisees too (e.g., Luke 7:36-50). Jesus was conscious that he was in the world on a mission which would never be fulfilled unless he mixed freely with those he had come to reach. In his prayer Jesus clearly shows that he intends his disciples to share his mission; for this purpose they are set apart by his truth.

Not of the world. Christians who live holy lives will soon discover that they do not fit in with the world—simply because they do not really belong here. As Jesus said of his disciples, "The world has hated them because they are not of the world" (Jn 17:14). Here again the Christian is simply following in the steps of the Master, for Jesus adds, "even as I

143

am not of the world."

The Christian is like an ambassador who lives in an alien land and whose very calling demands that he or she should do so. But the ambassador is under the authority of another government to which allegiance is owed. "Do not wonder, brethren, that the world hates you," wrote John (1 Jn 3:13), recalling no doubt the words of the Master which he had recorded in his Gospel. In the world a Christian is like a sojourner and a pilgrim (1 Pet 1:17; 2:11), and Christians who realize this will be utterly different from those around them.

Indeed, so opposed is the world to God that one cannot love them both at once. Christians at home in the world, following fashions and accommodating their standards to those around them, are in a very precarious condition. They ought to heed seriously the words of John, "If any one loves the world, love for the Father is not in him" (1 Jn 2:15), and the warning of James, "Do you not know that friendship with the world is enmity with God?" (Jas 4:4).

This is why a continual desire for worldly pleasures often signifies that all is not well. Some of this world's pleasures, even in moderation, will undermine a Christian's spiritual life. If a married man wants to flirt with other girls, even in moderation, one assumes that there is something wrong with his marriage—or if not, that there soon will be! So it is when a Christian flirts with worldliness. The command is clear and uncompromising:

Come out from them,
and be separate from them, says the Lord,
and touch nothing unclean;
then I will welcome you. (2 Cor 6:17)

We are to abstain from every form of evil (1 Thess 5:22).

So a Christian has to be in the world but not of it. Clearly the Christian course is going to involve us in unending conflict. We will find ourselves out in the middle of the stream. But we must swim against it and refuse to be carried along

144

with the current like a dead fish. We must do so to prove the vitality of our faith. We will engage in the good works which evidence faith's reality. "Religion that is pure and undefiled before God and the Father is this: to visit orphans and widows in their affliction, and to keep oneself unstained from the world" (Jas 1:27).

How do we become stained by the world? Paul says in Romans 12:2 that we are transformed by the renewal of our minds. To become stained we need merely do nothing, for stain will occur wherever the mind is unchanged, wherever we follow the natural assumptions of untransformed thinking.

Worldly ambition, for example, urges us to strive after status. Some will sacrifice anything to get to the top—their marriage, health and spiritual life. "What good is it for a man to gain the whole world, yet forfeit his soul?" (Mk 8:36 NIV). Or we may be dominated by the love of material luxury, and there is certainly plenty of opportunity for this today, especially in Western countries. Scripture has warned us that riches can hinder our spiritual lives, and many of us would be far better Christians if we opted for a simpler lifestyle. The love of pleasure and worldly amusement is a third common stumbling block, and for many, immediate gratification is the prime consideration. For others the approval of friends is what determines how they live. Jesus, however, warns his disciples: "Woe to you, when all men speak well of you, for so their fathers did to the false prophets" (Lk 6:26). Of course we should try to "commend ourselves to every man's conscience in the sight of God" (2 Cor 4:2), but we should never compromise our standards for the sake of popularity. God calls us to be different, to stand out in marked contrast to those around us without Christ. Only so can we be effective as Christians whom Jesus compared to salt, pointing out that if salt loses its distinctive tang "it is no longer good for anything" (Mt 5:13).

The Flesh

Our third foe, the flesh, is most relevant of all to the subject of sanctification. It brings before us the solemn facts of our own nature, that nature which the Holy Spirit is sanctifying.

"Flesh" can refer simply to the substance of our physical bodies and so to the earthly part of a person in contrast to the spirit. But here, as our foe, we mean by "flesh" what we are by nature apart from Christ. And we learn from Scripture that our flesh, in itself, is no help at all in the spiritual life. One who has only been "born of the flesh" cannot enter the kingdom of God (Jn 3:5-6). The flesh cannot help in things that pertain to the spirit, which is beyond its sphere. "It is the spirit that gives life, the flesh is of no avail" (Jn 6:63). As Jesus pointed out to Peter just after he had confessed that Jesus was the Christ, "Flesh and blood has not revealed this to you" (Mt 16:17). To understand the truth about Christ's Person, we need more than the natural faculties of the human brain.

The weakness of the flesh. Even after we have been born of the Spirit, our flesh hinders us by its very weakness. Jesus reminded Peter in the Garden of Gethsemane that "the spirit indeed is willing, but the flesh is weak" (Mt 26:41). Peter, with all his intentions of loyalty, was easily overcome by fatigue. Sometimes the expression *all flesh* is used to refer to the human race as a whole, especially with its weakness in contrast to God's power. The psalmist boasts, because he has put his trust in God, "What can flesh do to me?" (Ps 56:4).

It is because of the weakness of our flesh that law alone cannot produce salvation. As the apostle writes, God has done for us in Christ "what the law, weakened by the flesh, could not do" (Rom 8:3). Indeed, Paul says, "I delight in the law of God, in my inmost self" (Rom 7:22). Being in Christ he could recognize the truth and righteousness of God's law. But he also knew how his weak flesh hindered him actually putting into practice that law.

146

Its morally neutral nature. While our flesh is obviously a problem for us as we try to grow in sanctification, we must not suppose that the body is evil in itself. This error has historically led to two opposite and extreme views. On the one hand, the idea that the body is inherently evil and beyond redemption has led to unrestrained license; on the other, it has led to asceticism. Both, of course, are quite contrary to Scripture. God has created our flesh, the Incarnation affirms it, and the future resurrection promises its redemption.

But, morally neutral as it is, the flesh makes an easy foothold for the devil because of its weakness. Sin can take the perfectly natural, God-created functions of the body and turn them into "the lusts of the flesh." Eating and drinking can be turned into gluttony. Sex can be expressed in adultery, fornication and other sinful behavior. And sleep can become sloth. If we allow sin to reign in our mortal bodies, it will exploit our weakness and spoil our lives (Rom 6:12). This is why most of our sins or "works of the flesh" as Paul calls them, have a psychological element. Among those listed in Galatians 5:19-21, for example, we note that strife, jealousy and anger can arise through feelings of insecurity or inferiority—fleshly weaknesses.

Its conflict with the Spirit. The flesh as it is exploited by sin (and this is how Paul normally uses the word) is directly opposed to the Holy Spirit and all he is seeking to promote in a Christian's life. "The desires of the flesh are against the Spirit, and the desires of the Spirit are against the flesh; for these are opposed to each other" (Gal 5:17). When we face the command to let the Holy Spirit fill us, we experience the flesh with its desires standing in the way. Every Christian is constantly confronted with this choice: whether to submit to the control of the Holy Spirit, or to gratify his own selfish desires.

Other factors are at work on this spiritual battlefield too, as Paul describes in Romans 7. The law of God appeals to his mind: "I delight in the law of God, in my inmost self" (Rom 7:22). "The law is holy, and the commandment is holy and just and good" (Rom 7:12). Paul summarizes the whole conflict in the final verse of the chapter: "So then, I of myself serve the law of God with my mind, but with my flesh I serve the law of sin." He is torn between the two.

Sin, of course, wants to dominate the mind as well as the rest of our flesh. Paul speaks of the carnal mind (see Rom 8:5-8) and the sensuous mind (Col 2:18). Here the flesh is uppermost and dominates not only the actions but even the thinking that underlies them. Paul describes gentile Christians before their conversion as being like this when he recalls, "We all once lived in the passions of our flesh, following the desires of body and mind, and so we were by nature children of wrath, like the rest of mankind" (Eph 2:3).

Its sanctification. Here we have reasons for stressing the importance of the mind for the life of holiness besides those advanced in chapter eleven. I have heard it actually claimed by a speaker that the mind must be put aside for the Holy Spirit to work effectively. Nothing could be further from the truth. When the mind does not function, it is not the Holy Spirit who takes over but the flesh. The mind and the Holy Spirit are on the same side of the battle against the flesh, and the Holy Spirit needs the minds of Christians for them to understand and apply God's Word (cf. Rom 7:25 and Gal 5:17). Notice how Paul attributes the difficulties his readers have with his teaching—difficulties to which he accommodates his approach—not to intellectual weakness, but to the infirmity of their flesh (Rom 6:19 KJV, which is more literal than many modern renderings). If we cannot progress from milk to solid food because we choose not to exercise our minds, we should remember that laziness is a sin of the flesh.

The church at Corinth thought they were spiritual, but Paul had to say to them, "But I, brethren, could not address you as spiritual men, but as men of the flesh." Why? Not only because of their inability to take the solid food of God's Word, but also because of their jealousy and strife and other evidences of immaturity. The special danger for those who are ruled by their feelings is increased when living, as the Corinthians did, in a sensuous society. If, as is often the case, it is nothing more than the emotionally unstable not growing out of their immaturity, it is sad enough. But history has some more tragic examples of "spiritual" movements which began by putting aside the mind in favor of emotion, and led to the most appalling immoralities (helped on by the perfectionist assumptions we referred to on pages 78-81).

The Ultimate Foe

These, then, are the Christian's enemies. Our ultimate foe is the devil. The world around us presents both a sphere of service and a polluted atmosphere from which we must keep ourselves pure. But our greatest problem is the flesh, our own nature in which the enemy has obtained a foothold. However, the body is capable of sanctification. The flesh may be defiled (Jude 8), but it can also be purified (Heb 9:13). When Paul says that God purposes to sanctify us wholly, he goes on to include spirit and soul *and body* (1 Thess 5:23). The body is even described as "a temple of the Holy Spirit" (1 Cor 6:19). Romans 12:1 exhorts us to present our bodies as a living sacrifice, and in the next chapter we will see how we can go about this.

14
Mortification

The actual word mortify *occurs* only twice in the New Testament. It gets right to the heart of the conflict in which Christians who would present their bodies as sacrifice are involved. We are not merely fighting here against temptation as an external foe, but we are facing the realities of sin in our own nature. Two verses show this:

> If ye live after the flesh, ye shall die: but if ye through the Spirit do mortify the deeds of the body, ye shall live.
> (Rom 8:13 KJV)
> Put to death therefore what is earthly in you.
> (Col 3:5)

Two different words are used for *mortify* in these two verses, but there is no need to look for varying shades of meaning. Both of them mean "to exterminate life" or "to put to death."

They speak of a violent contest and may be compared to the cutting off of hands and plucking out of eyes in Mark 9:43-48. Notice, too, that it is a continuous activity; the use of the present tense in both these verses implies that Christians should be constantly mortifying the sin within them.

A missionary once had in his garden a shrub that bore poisonous leaves. At that time his small son would put everything within reach into his mouth. Naturally the missionary dug out the dangerous shrub; but the shrub had very deep roots which he could not quite reach, and it sprang up again. Although he repeatedly dug it up, it would always sprout once more. All he could do was to inspect the ground regularly, and every time the shrub appeared above the surface, dig it up again. Indwelling sin is like that shrub. It is a constant problem to Christians, and therefore mortification is always incumbent upon us. John Owen wisely said: "He who ceases from this duty, lets go all endeavours after holiness."[1]

We must be exercising it every day, and in every duty. Sin will not die, unless it be constantly weakened. Spare it, and it will heal its wounds, and recover its strength. We must continually watch against the operations of this principle of sin: in our duties, in our calling, in conversation, in retirement, in our straits, in our enjoyments, and in all that we do. If we are negligent on any occasion, we shall suffer by it; every mistake, every neglect is perilous.[2]

The Function of God's Law
God's law plays a vital part in our sanctification and in the mortifying of our sinful nature.[3] In Romans 7:7-13 Paul shows what the law meant to him before he became a Christian. Then in verse 14 the tense changes from the past to the present, and Paul goes on to tell what it means to him now as a Christian. Paul is not speaking of any lower state of Christian experience which he had left behind. He is writing as one who has learned to "delight in the law of God, in my inmost

self" (v. 22). Paul is writing here out of a mature experience of God's grace. As Handley Moule observed, "He who can truly speak thus of an inmost sympathy, a sympathy of delight, with the most holy law of God, is no half-Christian; certainly not in St. Paul's view of things."[4]

What the law cannot do. Much as we may glory in God's law, however, we must never lose sight of its limitations. Not that there is anything inadequate about God's law in itself; it is in men that the inadequacy lies—to use Paul's words, it was "weakened by the flesh" (Rom 8:3). Because of this, a set of rules, even from God himself, can neither justify nor sanctify.

In *Pilgrim's Progress,* Christian very early in his journey discovered that the law cannot justify. He learned this the hard way, foolishly following Mr. Worldly Wiseman's advice; he turned away from the road to the cross which he had been treading to call at Mr. Legality's house on Mount Sinai.

So Christian turned out of his way to go to Mr. Legality's house for help; but, behold, when he was got now hard by the hill, it seemed so high, and also that side of it that was next the wayside did hang so much over, that Christian was afraid to venture further, lest the hill should fall on his head; wherefore there he stood still, and wotted not what to do. Also his burden now seemed heavier to him as he set him again on the right road. "No man was as yet ever rid of his burden by him; no, nor ever is like to be: ye cannot be justified by the works of the law."

We cannot in our weak flesh climb the mountain of God's rules; in fact, the more perfect his law, the more despair we experience in facing it. "A man is not justified by works of the law" (Gal 2:16).

Nor can the law sanctify the believer. It can even have the opposite effect: "But sin, finding opportunity in the commandment, wrought in me all kinds of covetousness. Apart from the law sin lies dead. I was once alive apart from the law, but when the commandment came, sin revived and I died" (Rom 7:8-9). Through the weakness of human flesh, the very law of God himself "which promised life proved to be death to me" (Rom 7:10). Paul's observation is very realistic. A prohibition can indeed be very provocative, and the command "Thou shalt not" can produce an irresistible urge toward "But I will"; it can hardly be described as having a sanctifying effect!

Our hero in *Pilgrim's Progress* had this further lesson to learn, and he did so in Interpreter's House. He was taken into a large room full of dust. When a man began to sweep, the dust rose into the air and almost choked him. Before the room could be cleaned, water had to be sprinkled to keep the dust down. Interpreter explained:

This parlour is the heart of a man that was never sanctified by the sweet grace of the Gospel; the dust is his original sin, and inward corruptions, that have defiled the whole man. He that began to sweep at first, is the Law; but she that brought water, and did sprinkle it, is the Gospel. Now, whereas thou sawest, that so soon as the first began to sweep, the dust did so fly about that the room by him could not be cleansed, but that thou wast almost choked therewith; this is to show thee, that the law, instead of cleansing the heart [by its working] from sin, doth revive, put strength into, and increase it in the soul, even as it doth discover and forbid it, for it doth not give power to subdue.

So Paul could say, "The power of sin is the law" (1 Cor 15:56), for unless it is accompanied by the gospel, the law is precisely what chokes our lives.

Why is God's law unable to achieve either our justification or sanctification? The answer we give is no mere academic one, but is vital to a life of holiness. To use Paul's expression, the law was weakened by the flesh; that is, there is nothing deficient in the law itself: the weakness is in us. Paul confessed his own bitter experience of failure in Romans 7:14-23.

Repeatedly he finds himself powerless to perform the very law of God in which he delights. At last he cries out in anguish, "Wretched man that I am! Who will deliver me from this body of death?" (v. 24). And Paul's burden is not made any lighter by knowing the seriousness of sin and its tragic consequences.

What the law can and must do. We can see now the important role which God's law must play in our sanctification. Although it can never sanctify, it provides us an indispensable incentive for mortifying our sinful natures. As Herbert W. Cragg commented at the 1963 Keswick Convention:

Paul has discovered something which is absolutely fundamental to holy living. He has discovered, I believe, that this outcry of distress is written into the very fabric of a holy life. It is not a crisis to pass; it is part of the very fabric of holiness. He never looked at himself without shame, from which he turns in loathing to look again on Christit.[5]

Here is one of the marks of growth in grace: not extravagant claims to victory, but a loathing of the sinful nature that remains.

John R. W. Stott has also commented pointedly on this theme in Romans 7.

Indeed, an honest and humble acknowledgment of the hopeless evil of our flesh, even after the new birth, is the first step to holiness. To speak quite plainly, some of us are not leading holy lives for the simple reason that we have too high an opinion of ourselves. No man ever cries aloud for deliverance who has not seen his own wretchedness. In other words, the only way to arrive at faith in the power of the Holy Spirit is along the road of self-despair. No device exists to settle this issue for good. The power and subtlety of the flesh are such that we dare not relax one moment. The only hope is unremitting vigilance and dependence.[6]

"Load thy conscience with the guilt of [sin]," demands John

Owen. "Bring the holy law of God into thy conscience, lay thy corruption to it, pray that thou mayest be affected with it."[7]

The Function of Gospel

We have already seen that the death of Christ is the only ground on which a person defiled by sin can be set apart for God.[8] John Owens has called it the "meritorious cause" of our mortification as well, for it shows us what should be the Christian's attitude to his sin.

Again we turn to the book of Romans. Chapter 6 begins with Paul anticipating a common objection to his gospel of free forgiveness—and especially his expression of it in the closing two verses of chapter 5. Indeed if, as he has just stated, "where sin increased, grace abounded all the more," it would seem that the more we sin the more we experience God's grace. Does this mean, he asks, that we can continue a life of sin because forgiveness is so easy?

Emphatically not. A proper understanding of the death and resurrection of Christ and the believer's intimate relationship with them must result in a denial of such a suggestion. A Christian is in personal union with Christ, a state inwardly created by faith and outwardly signified by baptism, in which Christ's death is reckoned as the Christian's death. It is as if the Christian had suffered death, the penalty for sin. Because of this, sin and its penalty have no further claim on him or her. Because such a person has shown the attitude of God toward his past sinful life, he can and must regard this as a closed book.[9]

How this relates to mortification we can see in the three logical steps of verse 6. The New English Bible translation is especially helpful here: "We know that the man we once were has been crucified with Christ, for the destruction of the sinful self, so that we may no longer be the slaves of sin." "The man we once were" is a fitting rendering of "our old man"

(KJV), for this can hardly be the same thing as "the body of sin" (KJV), which comes later in the same sentence. Colossians uses the expression "our old man" similarly to mean the old pattern of life which the believer had followed in his or her pre-Christian days, a pattern which is now gone. Holy living is demanded of Christians on the assumption that they have "put off the old nature with its practices" (Col 3:9). On what ground does Paul make this assumption? It is given in Romans 6:6: "Our old self was crucified with him." Christ paid the penalty for our old way of life, and Christians, when they believe Christ, made that death their own.

Now, Paul goes on, the purpose of this death was that "the sinful body might be destroyed." We know from other occurrences of this word in the New Testament that this does not mean our sinful nature is completely eradicated. Rather, its power is broken. This in turn means "that we may no longer be the slaves of sin" (NEB).

All this happened to our sins when Christ died. Now in verse 11 Paul says, "Consider yourselves dead to sin." In other words, we should accept the fact and live accordingly. Of course, there is a paradox here, as F. F. Bruce points out.

This apparent paradox is one that we meet repeatedly in the Pauline writings, where believers are enjoined time and again to be what they are—to be in actual practice what they are as members of Christ. Thus they are said to "have put off the old man with his deeds" and to "have put on the new man" (Col 3:9f.), while elsewhere they are exhorted to "put off . . . the old man" and "put on the new man" (Eph 4:22, 24).[10]

In the same way Paul calls Christians to crucify sin's two allies, the flesh and the world:

And those who belong to Christ Jesus have crucified the flesh with its passions and desires. (Gal 5:24)

But far be it from me to glory except in the cross of our Lord Jesus Christ, by which the world has been crucified

157

to me, and I to the world. (Gal 6:14)

In the first of these the crucifying is something the Christian has done, rather than something which has been done to him. The basic idea, however, is the same. Paul assumes by using the past tense that his readers, by virtue of their relation to Christ, have shared God's attitude toward their sin, the flesh and the world in which they live. For a Christian to live a life dominated by the flesh or in fellowship with the world is a denial of his or her very relationship to a crucified Christ. The second verse underscores this.

Christians who are growing in their love for Jesus Christ are increasingly influenced by what their salvation cost. Aware that they have been "bought with a price," they feel the obligation to glorify God in their bodies (1 Cor 6:20). Let me state it the other way round: the more Christians consider what their sin cost the Savior, the more they will shrink from it.

Bring thy lust to the Gospel,—not for relief, but for further conviction of its guilt; look on Him whom thou hast pierced, and be in bitterness. Say to thy soul "What have I done? What love, what mercy, what blood, what grace have I despised and trampled on! Is this the return I make to the Father for His love, to the Son for His blood, to the Holy Ghost for His grace?"[11]

The Way of Mortification

To mortify our indwelling sin is constantly to weaken it. We can do this in three ways: starve it out, cut it out or crowd it out. The world today offers plenty to feed a person's sinful nature, such as periodicals, books, movies, television programs and even conversations. We have to remember that indwelling sin is nourished in the mind with its thoughts and imagination. It is there that our jealousies, resentments, lusts and selfishness are fostered. We can begin mortifying sin in us by depriving the mind—starving it—of the foods that feed its cancer. If there are pleasures, relationships or environments which add to our temptations, we shall wherever possible avoid them.

Sin also has to be cut out, just as the poisonous shrub had to be dug out every time it reappeared. Sin must be denied every opportunity for expression, or as Paul put it, we must "make no provision for the flesh, to gratify its desires" (Rom 13:14). Where sin does reassert itself, we must admit it, confess it and renounce it by the Spirit's help.

This is no easy undertaking, and we need to be realistic about it.

> Some look upon it as an easy task. But is it for nothing that the Holy Spirit expresses it by mortification, or killing? Certainly this intimates a violent contest. Everything will do its utmost to preserve its life. Let no man think to kill sin with a few gentle strokes. He, who has once smitten the serpent, if he follow not his blow till it be slain, may repent that ever he began the quarrel; and so will he who undertakes to deal with sin, if he pursue it not constantly to death; sin will revive, and the man must die.[12]

Despite what some have taught, this is the proper attitude toward our sinful nature. It is far removed from the repression of which psychologists have warned us. The latter involves a refusal to face even the possibility of sin. "I am not the kind of person to do that, because I am not tempted in that way" expresses an attitude of repression. Mortification means that a Christian says, "I am the kind of person who can do that very sin, but by the grace of God I will not do it."

At the very heart of mortification is the denial of self. In our *selves* we find the very heart of sin: rebellion against God, putting self on the throne of one's life instead of him. It is self that spoils people's lives again and again, and it can even intrude into religious activity. How often Christian fellowship has been marred or ruined by petty squabbling, at the bottom of which lay an uncrucified self. Such strife and division were the symptoms of the carnality of the Corinthian Christians (1 Cor 3:3). Little wonder that Jesus enjoins any would-be disciple, "Let him deny himself" (Mt 16:24).

The third way to mortify our sinful nature is to strangle it with whatever is good and beautiful. A piece of wasteland soon becomes covered with weeds and wild grass. A well-planted garden, however, although still needing attention, has less room for weeds. The Bible encourages a Christian to be positive, even in the matter of mortification: "Walk by the Spirit, and do not gratify the desires of the flesh" (Gal 5:16). As Christians live in fellowship with the Holy Spirit of God and foster in their lives the things that please him, so the less worthy things are crowded out. Or, as John R. W. Stott puts it, mortification is to be accompanied by aspiration.[13]

John Owen calls this "the weakening of the flesh by the growth of positive graces," and he observes that every sin has a corresponding virtue by which it can be displaced. "So by the implanting and growth of humility is pride weakened, passion by patience, uncleanness by purity of mind and conscience, love of this world by heavenly-mindedness."[14] Ephesians 4:22-32 describes this transaction graphically. The apostle tells us what to "put off" side by side with what corresponding virtues to "put on." For example, a Christian is not only to refrain from stealing, but, "Let him labor, doing honest work with his hands, so that he may be able to give to those in need" (v. 28). In other words, we are not to have holes where sin used to be, but godly virtues.

One of the ways in which a Christian can be positive is in the way that he feeds his thought life. "As he thinketh in his heart, so is he" (Prov 23:7 KJV). Having "starved" our minds of what would tempt us to sin, we need to feed it with what tends to righteousness. The Christian mind is filled with what is lovely. Let us affirm the well-known advice of the apostle Paul in this connection: "Finally, brethren, whatever is true, whatever is honorable, whatever is just, whatever is pure, whatever is lovely, whatever is gracious, if there is any excellence, if there is anything worthy of praise, think about these things" (Phil 4:8).

The Hope of Victory

We must be realistic about the Christian life. In doing so we must acknowledge the severity of the conflict in which Christians are involved, the subtlety of the foe that we face and the extreme difficulty of the mortification that God commands us to undertake. However, we must not imagine that this is a hopeless struggle.

Satan may indeed be a subtle and deadly foe, but we must remind ourselves of the promise that "where sin increased, grace abounded all the more" (Rom 5:20). We must echo Paul's defiant cry, "If God is for us, who is against us?" (Rom 8:31). The fight of the Christian against the world, the flesh and the devil is not like the hopeless struggle of the unregenerate person who is still under sin's bondage. The Christian certainly has to fight sin day by day, and sometimes it will get the better of him, but no longer does "sin... reign in your mortal bodies, to make you obey their passions" (Rom 6:12).

Sin in the Christian is no longer master. The devil is already a defeated foe; his doom was settled forever by the death and resurrection of Jesus Christ. If we decide to mortify sin in our lives and do it by the Spirit, we have the assurance of God's Word that we will live (Rom 8:13). In our hope lies much incentive.

15
Journey's
End

We will not go on forever growing in holiness. The process of sanctification will one day be complete. The fight will
be over and the Christian's enemies completely destroyed.
It will happen when this life is ended and when the course
of history reaches its consummation at the second coming
of Christ. Most of God's people enter the final stage in their
salvation through death, but some, those who are still alive
at Christ's coming, will be transformed and glorified at that
time.

Glorification
What is this coming "glorification" for the Christian? The
word *glorification* relates to sanctification in several ways. In

one sense it is the final stage in sanctification. Negatively, the mortification of sin will be complete and sin will be finally uprooted from the Christian's nature, for we will be "without blemish" (Jude 24). Positively, the Christian will be like Christ (1 Jn 3:2). At last we will be thoroughly conformed to the image of God's Son. This is the goal toward which the present sanctifying activity of the Holy Spirit is working.

When we are glorified, the careful distinction we drew in chapter seven between justification and sanctification will no longer apply. As Richard Hooker has put it, "The righteousness wherewith we shall be clothed in the world to come is both perfect and inherent; that whereby we are here justified is perfect but not inherent; that whereby we are sanctified, inherent, but not perfect." It is an error of perfectionism to confuse sanctification and glorification. Entire sanctification is certainly taught in Scripture, but it will not be realized until the coming of Jesus Christ. This is clearly implied by the apostle Paul: "May the God of peace himself sanctify you wholly; and may your spirit and soul and body be kept sound and blameless at the coming of our Lord Jesus Christ" (1 Thess 5:23).

Another mistake is to separate the two doctrines. Sanctification, we are sometimes told, is salvation from the power of sin, whereas glorification will be salvation from the presence of sin. This could be a misleading half-truth. Sanctification does not merely consist in keeping the sinful nature under control, although it certainly includes that. Rather, it involves an inward work of the Holy Spirit whereby we are being transformed into the very likeness of Christ, and our inward sinful nature is being mortified. It is the very process of which glorification is the final stage.

The Bible often uses the word *salvation* for this process, with the verb *save* in the future tense (see, e.g., Mt 24:13). Looking forward to that great day, Paul says, "Salvation is nearer to us now than when we first believed" (Rom 13:11). When Christ comes again, "Unto them that look for him shall he appear the second time without sin unto salvation" (Heb 9:28 KJV). As Michael Green commented when speaking at the Keswick Convention in 1964, "Sometimes we sing hymns about full salvation. This is not true. We have not got full salvation now. That belongs to the future."[1]

This salvation will involve the complete defeat of all the Christian's enemies. Instead of the sinful world in which the Christian has now to live, there will be "new heavens and a new earth in which righteousness dwells" (2 Pet 3:13). As for the devil himself, he will be thrown into the lake of fire (Rev 20:10), while the Christian, to use the words of the Prayer Book Burial Service, will be delivered from "the burden of the flesh." No longer will the Christian be dragged down by the weakness of his or her flesh.

In *Pilgrim's Progress* we see Christian and Hopeful, after passing through the river of death, climbing up the hill toward the Celestial City with ease. The toil and the striving which they had known during their earthly pilgrimage is gone because now "they had left their mortal garments behind them in the river." Not that we look forward to a disembodied state, but rather we will have bodies glorified and completely freed from the limitations and the weakness of our mortal flesh (see 1 Cor 15:50-52; 2 Cor 5:1-4).

The Blessed Hope

A word that is frequently used in connection with the final consummation of our salvation is *hope*. Not only do Christians look back to the cross and upward to Christ enthroned, but we also look forward to the day when we will stand before him. In this hope we are saved (Rom 8:24), and Paul describes the event itself as "our blessed hope" (Tit 2:13).

Now the common usage of this word does not convey at all its biblical meaning. Often it expresses uncertainty; the expression "I hope so" immediately conveys an impression of doubt. Nothing could be further removed from the meaning of this word in the Bible, for there it expresses complete certainty. Where the sanctifying work of the Holy Spirit is proceeding in Christian lives, they can be absolutely sure that that work will be completed. Here is the confidence that Paul expressed to the Philippians: "And I am sure that he who began a good work in you will bring it to completion at the day of Jesus Christ" (Phil 1:6). He assures the Thessalonians of their entire sanctification, saying, "He who calls you is faithful, and he will do it" (1 Thess 5:24). We can no more separate sanctification from glorification than we can sanctification from justification. If God is now at work in our lives, we can be quite sure that he will complete the job. "Those whom he justified he also glorified" (Rom 8:30). God's work is never an unfinished symphony.

So the present work of the Holy Spirit is a guarantee of its completion. Indeed, Paul refers to the Holy Spirit as "the earnest of our inheritance," for the Greek word for "earnest" meant a deposit or first installment of a payment pledging more to follow. Here we have one of the greatest incentives to holy living. Material things are only temporary, and the world and the flesh with all their apparent pleasures will pass away. Holy living is the only pursuit really worth following. "Since all these things are thus to be dissolved, what sort of persons ought you to be in lives of holiness and godliness" (2 Pet 3:11), remarks Peter. If we truly grasp our hope for the future, we will work for it right now in cooperation with the Holy Spirit. "Every one who thus hopes in him," wrote John, "purifies himself as he is pure" (1 Jn 3:3).

Work on, then, Lord, till on my soul
    Eternal light shall break,
And, in Thy likeness perfected,
    I "satisfied" shall wake.
        E. H. H.

Notes

Chapter 1: The Way of Holiness
[1]James Philip, *Christian Maturity* (London: Inter-Varsity Fellowship, 1964), p. 70.
[2]Charles H. Spurgeon, *The Treasury of the Bible*, III (London: Marshall, Morgan & Scott, 1962), p. 277.
[3]In the New Testament there are two additional Greek adjectives occasionally used for *holy*.
[4]John Owen, *On the Holy Spirit* (1674; reprinted, Edinburgh: Banner of Truth, 1966), p. 220.

Chapter 2: The Holiness of God
[1]Rudolf Otto, *The Idea of the Holy*, trans. J. W. Harvey (London: Oxford University Press, 1946).
[2]C. S. Lewis, *The Problem of Pain* (New York: Macmillan, 1962), p. 17.
[3]Stephen C. Neill, *Christian Holiness* (Guildford, England: Lutterworth, 1960), p. 19.
[4]R. A. Finlayson, *The Holiness of God* (Glasgow: Pickering and Inglis, 1955), p. 4.
[5]L. Berkhof, *Systematic Theology* (Edinburgh: Banner of Truth, 1959), p. 74.
[6]For example, Is 29:13, where again the word *honor* is the word translated "sanctify" elsewhere.
[7]William McDougall, *An Introduction to Social Psychology* (New York: Methuen, 1908), p. 132.

Chapter 3: A Holy People
[1]Incidentally, it is in connection with the Sabbath that the word *holy* is first used in Scripture (Gen 2:3).
[2]For examples of this use of *holy*, see Lk 1:70; Eph 3:5; 2 Pet 1:21.

Chapter 4: Sin
[1]John C. Ryle, *Holiness* (Cambridge: James Clarke, 1952), p. 1.
[2]Ernest F. Kevan, *Keep His Commandments* (London: Tyndale Press, 1964), p. 16.

[3]Ryle, *Holiness*, p. 3.
[4]Philip, *Christian Maturity*, p. 43.
[5]Ibid.

Chapter 5: The Means of Sanctification

[1]Owen, *On the Holy Spirit*, p. 223.
[2]B. B. Warfield, *Perfectionism* (Phillipsburg, N.J.: Presbyterian and Reformed Publishing Co., 1958), pp. 397-98.
[3]Ibid., p. 398.
[4]I hasten to add that Paul is writing here of the Christian who is already married to a non-Christian when he or she is converted. There is no excuse here for a union between a believer and an unbeliever subsequent to conversion. In such cases the command of God is clear: "Do not be mismated with unbelievers" (2 Cor 6:14).
[5]Alan M. Stibbs, *First Epistle of Peter*, Tyndale New Testament Commentary (Grand Rapids: Eerdmans, 1959), p. 72.
[6]Robert Haldane, *The Epistle to the Romans* (Edinburgh: Banner of Truth, 1959), p. 620.
[7]Harry A. Ironside, *Holiness: The False and the True* (Glasgow: Pickering and Inglis, 1935), p. 57.
[8]Berkhof, *Systematic Theology*, p. 535.
[9]Charles Kingsley Barrett, *The Gospel according to St. John* (London: SPCK, 1956), p. 426.

Chapter 6: Progressive Sanctification—Renewal

[1]It is true that, grammatically, the "renewal in the Holy Spirit" could be taken as synonymous with "the washing of regeneration." Donald Guthrie faces these two possibilities of interpretation, and we agree with his conclusions for the reasons he gives: "The 'regeneration' and the 'renewing' may be regarded as distinct operations, or both may be dependent on 'washing' and therefore would describe different aspects of one operation. But since regeneration must always precede the process of renewal and since renewal is never described elsewhere as a washing, the former interpretation is to be preferred" (Donald Guthrie, *The Pastoral Epistles*, Tyndale New Testament Commentary [Grand Rapids: Eerdmans, 1957], p. 206).
[2]The theory we are denying here has been known as "counteraction" and was taught by some speakers in the earlier years of the Keswick movement. In rejecting the perfectionist idea of eradication, the view that a Christian's sinful nature can be completely and finally removed during this present life, it went to the other extreme and taught that one's

sinful nature remains unchanged throughout life. The way of sanctification consists in keeping the sinful nature under control by reckoning
that it is dead. At the heart of this theory is a particular interpretation of
Romans 6 and especially verse 6. For a helpful study of this passage, see
John R. W. Stott, *Men Made New* (Downers Grove, Ill.: InterVarsity Press,
1981), pp. 31-57.
[3]Charles Hodge, *Systematic Theology*, III (Cambridge: James Clarke,
1960), p. 214.
[4]John Owen, *Temptation and Sin* (Grand Rapids: Zondervan, 1959), p. 20.

Chapter 7: Sanctification and Justification

[1]As we saw in chapter five, sanctification, both in the Epistle to the Hebrews and in the writings of Paul, *includes* an aspect which is positional,
objective and external. For this reason we must recognize that the use of
the word *sanctify* in the Epistle to the Hebrews brings it very close in
meaning to justification. This does not mean, however, that in Hebrews
the word can simply be included under the heading of justification. The
latter is the language of the law courts and has to do with our legal standing, but *sanctify* is from the language of Old Testament worship and relates to purity. Also we have to remember that Paul, too, speaks of positional sanctification in, for example, his reference to all Christians as
"saints," irrespective of their progress in practical sanctification. This
does not mean that for him it was just a synonym for justification!

The important point for Paul is this: Although sanctification is essentially inward, progressive and experiential, it is based on the objective
work of Christ just as much as justification. So Christ is "made our . . .
righteousness" [i.e., justification] "and sanctification . . ." (1 Cor 1:30).
[2]Ludwig Ott, *Fundamentals of Catholic Dogma* (Mercier Press, 1955), p.
250.
[3]What we have described is the traditional view of the Roman Catholic
Church. While it has discussed the topic considerably in recent years,
the Roman Catholic Church does not appear to have changed its official
policy.
[4]See Romans 3:24-31 and the example of Abraham in Romans 4.
[5]Warfield, *Perfectionism*, p. 100.
[6]T. C. Hammond, *The New Creation* (London: Marshall, Morgan and Scott,
1953), p. 151.

Chapter 8: Perfectionism

[1]Charles G. Finney, *Systematic Theology* (1851), p. 407; italics mine.
[2]Gwyn Walters, *The New Bible Dictionary* (London: Inter-Varsity Fellow-

ship, 1962), p. 1141.

[3]Warfield, *Perfectionism*, pp. 39-40.

[4]Neill, *Christian Holiness*, p. 31.

[5]John R. W. Stott, *The Epistles of John*, Tyndale New Testament Commentary (Grand Rapids: Eerdmans, 1964), p. 168.

[6]Berkhof, *Systematic Theology*, p. 539.

[7]E. M. Blaiklock, *Keswick Week*, 1959, pp. 92-93.

[8]Neill, *Christian Holiness*, p. 35.

[9]Warfield, *Perfectionism*, p. 368.

[10]Handley C. G. Moule, *Philippian Studies* (Glasgow: Pickering and Inglis, 1956), p. 188.

[11]Neill, *Christian Holiness*, p. 37.

[12]Warfield, *Perfectionism*, p. 279; italics his.

[13]Ibid., pp. 279-80.

[14]Hannah Pearsall Smith, *The Christian's Secret of a Happy Life* (Welwyn Garden City, England: Nisbet, 1888), p. 36.

[15]Warfield, *Perfectionism*, p. 305.

[16]Neill, *Christian Holiness*, p. 38.

[17]G. C. Berkouwer, *Faith and Sanctification*, Studies in Dogmatics: Theology, vol. 1 (Grand Rapids: Eerdmanns, 1952), p. 49.

[18]Neill, *Christian Holiness*, p. 27.

Chapter 9: Christian Growth

[1]Hammond, *New Creation*, pp. 151-52.

[2]Stibbs, *1 Peter*, p. 73.

[3]Ryle, *Holiness*, p. 88.

[4]John C. Ryle, *Five Christian Leaders of the Eighteenth Century* (Edinburgh: Banner of Truth, 1960), p. 147.

[5]Berkhof, *Systematic Theology*, p. 537.

[6]Herbert W. Cragg, *The Conqueror's Way* (London: Inter-Varsity Fellowship, 1949), p. 23.

[7]Moule, *Philippian Studies*, p. 189.

[8]Owen, *On the Holy Spirit*, p. 237.

[9]Ibid.

[10]Thomas Watson, *A Body of Divinity* (Edinburgh: Banner of Truth, 1958), p. 4.

Chapter 10: Stimulants to Growth

[1]Owen, *On the Holy Spirit*, p. 238.

[2]Samuel Chadwick, *The Call to Christian Perfection* (London: Epworth Press, 1926), pp. 68ff.

³Ryle, *Holiness*, p. xv.

⁴Philip, *Christian Maturity*, p. 58.

⁵Ibid., p. 59.

⁶It is worth mentioning that G. C. Neal in an article, "In the Original Greek," published in the *Tyndale House Bulletin*, April 1963, has strongly questioned the whole idea of what he calls "the supposed distinction between the present and aorist tenses of the Greek verb in the infinitive, imperative, and subjunctive."

⁷Philip, *Christian Maturity*, pp. 56-57.

⁸This truth seems to have made a big impact on some of the early leaders of the Keswick movement.

⁹D. Martyn Lloyd-Jones, *Authority* (London: Inter-Varsity Fellowship, 1958), p. 78.

¹⁰For a treatment of this, see John R. W. Stott, *The Baptism and Fullness of the Holy Spirit*, 2nd edition (Downers Grove, Ill.: InterVarsity Press, 1975).

¹¹Stott, *Baptism and Fullness*, p. 50.

Chapter 11: The Fullness of the Holy Spirit

¹Stott, *Baptism and Fullness*, p. 60.

²See page 54.

³Stott, *Baptism and Fullness*, p. 56.

⁴D. Martyn Lloyd-Jones, *Life in the Spirit in Marriage, Home & Work* (Edinburgh: Banner of Truth, 1974), p. 20.

⁵James I. Packer, *Guidance and Wisdom* (London: Evangelical Press, undated), p. 5.

⁶Bernard Mobbs, *Our Rebel Emotions* (Sevenoaks, England: Hodder & Stoughton, 1970), p. 113.

⁷John R. W. Stott, *God's New Society* (Downers Grove, Ill.: InterVarsity Press, 1979), p. 208.

⁸It must be emphasized that the foregoing chapter is not intended to be a complete treatment of the work of the Holy Spirit, but only to deal with its relationship to holiness and sanctification. There are helpful books devoted entirely to the Holy Spirit, such as the following: Leon Morris, *Spirit of the Living God* (Downers Grove, Ill.: InterVarsity Press, 1960); John R. W. Stott, *Baptism and Fullness*.

Chapter 12: Faith and Effort

¹This expression seems to have been first used by C. H. A. Trumbull in a tract entitled *What is your kind of Christianity?* He used it to distinguish between surrender and faith and maintained that we may "let go" and

yet not "let God." So the surrendered life is not necessarily a victorious life. These two categories seem to come from Trumbull's imagination rather than from Scripture.

[2]Smith, *Christian's Secret*, p. 34.

[3]Ibid.; p. 35.

[4]D. Martyn Lloyd-Jones, *Christ Our Sanctification* (London: Inter-Varsity Fellowship, 1948), p. 18.

[5]This is the picture we are given of the Christian life in *Pilgrim's Progress*. There is very little suggestion there that it is simply a matter of ceasing from struggling and striving. Christian had to face Giant Despair in Doubting Castle, to fight with Apollyon and to climb the hill called Difficulty, to mention just a few of his experiences.

[6]See pp. 87-90.

Chapter 13: The Christian's Enemies

[1]Leon Morris, *New Bible Dictionary* (Inter-Varsity Fellowship, 1962), p. 1147.

Chapter 14: Mortification

[1]Owen, *On the Holy Spirit*, p. 307.

[2]Ibid., p. 310.

[3]A careful study of Romans 7 and the chapters surrounding it would be a great aid to understanding this entire theme, especially with the help of John R. W. Stott's most enlightening exposition of these chapters in *Men Made New*.

[4]Handley C. G. Moule, *The Epistle to the Romans* (Glasgow: Pickering and Inglis, 1956), p. 192.

[5]Herbert W. Cragg, *Keswick Week*, 1963, p. 51.

[6]Stott, *Men Made New*, p. 74.

[7]Owen, *Temptation and Sin*, pp. 56-57.

[8]See pp. 43-44.

[9]See Stott, *Men Made New*, p. 31, for a complete exposition of this passage.

[10]F. F. Bruce, *Romans*, Tyndale New Testament Commentary (Grand Rapids: Eerdmans, 1963), p. 44.

[11]Owen, *Temptation and Sin*, p. 58.

[12]Owen, *On the Holy Spirit*, p. 311.

[13]Stott, *Men Made New*, pp. 91-92.

[14]Owen, *Temptation and Sin*, p. 32.

Chapter 15: Journey's End

[1]Michael Green, *Keswick Week*, 1964, p. 131.